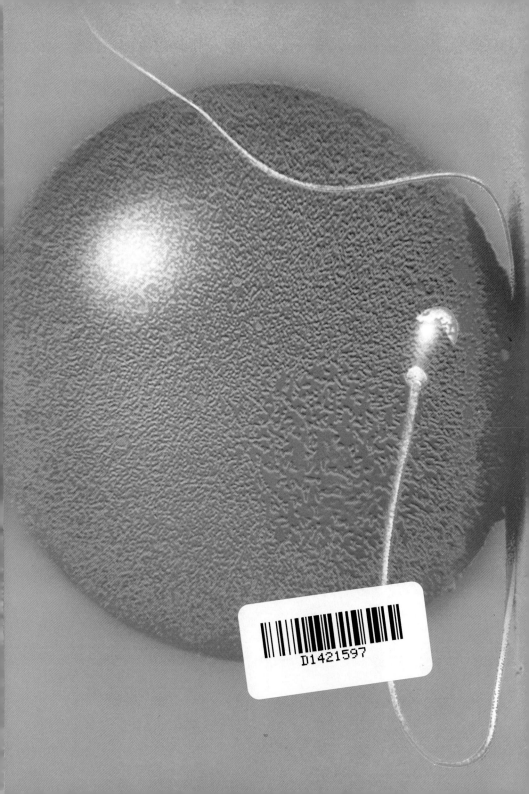

Thames & Hudson

THE BODY

Photoworks of the Human Form

WILLIAM A. EWING

with 366 illustrations,
35 in colour, 331 in duotone

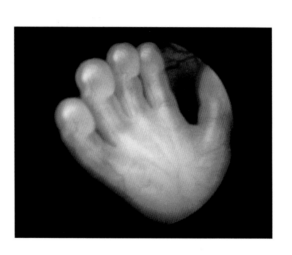

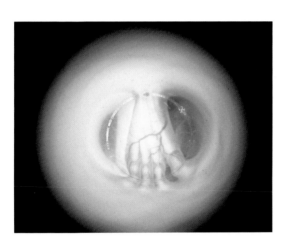

For Clare

p. 1
Dr David Phillips
A single spermatozoon fertilizing a human egg 1992
Scanning electron micrograph (SEM)

pp. 2-3
Arno Rafael Minkkinen
Abbaye de Montmajour, Arles 1983
Gelatin silver print
Courtesy: The artist, Andover, Massachusetts, USA

p. 4
Anonymous
Endoscopic image of the hand of a human foetus *in vivo* after 3 months 1985
Colour transparency

p. 5
Alexander Tsiaras
Endoscopic image of the foot of a human foetus *in vivo* after 11 weeks 1991
Colour transparency

First published in the United Kingdom in 1994 by Thames & Hudson Ltd,
181A High Holborn, London WC1V 7QX

British Library Cataloguing-in-Publication Data
A catalogue record for this book is available from the British Library

ISBN 0-500-27781-8

Printed and bound in Singapore by C.S. Graphics

CONTENTS

PREFACE

Why is it today that the human body is at the centre of so much attention? Why are magazines, newspapers, television and advertisements saturated with images of naked, or virtually naked, bodies? Why are so many writers, artists and photographers so profoundly concerned with the subject? And why, in all this, do we discern a rising tide of unease, even panic? Is it, as many believe, the scourge of AIDS which fuels the concern, or perhaps the disembodiment implicit in the computer age? Is it, as some academics maintain, that the body, as we have come to understand it, no longer exists? Or could it even be that the body is merely 'in fashion'?

What puts the body squarely in the centre of debate is not fashion, but urgency. The body is being rethought and reconsidered by artists and writers because it is being restructured and reconstituted by scientists and engineers. In an era when parts can be routinely detached from one body and plugged into another; when the U.S. National Institutes of Health offer to replace corpses in medical schools with 'industry-standard digital cadavers'; when certain machines can appropriate the functions of human organs, while others are invested with intelligence; when the life of the body can be prolonged when the mind has ceased to function; when genetic change can be engineered and human beings cloned; when a foetus can be nurtured in an artificial womb, or jobbed-out to a surrogate mother; when we entrust automatons to land our jets or perform operations on our bodies; when the *New York Times* informs us that, contrary to what most of us had believed, there are three, four or possibly five genders; when we capriciously

Arnulf Rainer
Strauch + Zack (Bush + Rick-Rack) 1971
Indian ink, oil crayon/photograph

9

rebuild faces, breasts or thighs to conform to the moment's ideal of beauty; and when we dream of 'Robocops', 'Terminators' and 'Replicants', and long to live in a *virtual* reality – then concepts and definitions, values and beliefs, rights and laws, must be radically overhauled. 'The binaries in modern thought are breaking down', notes Alice Jardine, 'and the bottom-line binary of traditional ethics – life and death – is falling out from under us.'[1] Jardine might well have listed the other threatened binaries: male/female, masculine/feminine, young/old, nature/culture, black/white... 'YOUR BODY IS A BATTLEGROUND,' a work by artist Barbara Kruger emphatically reminds us.

Photographers know all too well how easily their work can catapult them into the battles raging over the human body. Witness the storms of controversy which have surrounded the imagery of Robert Mapplethorpe, Sally Mann, Jock Sturges or Andres Serrano in recent years; it is always some perceived transgression of conventional notions of the body, particularly issues relating to sexuality, that ignites public passions.

Photography has had a profound impact on the body for more than a century. But while it has undoubtedly been of service to humankind, it is equally true that it has been the cause of much concern. It may be argued, for instance, that pornographic imagery has contributed to the degradation of the body, both female and male, or that advertising's glorification of wholly idealized youth sets up unrealistic expectations which alienate the common person from his/her own corporeality. But who would deny that medical photography has led us towards a fuller understanding of the body, and thus contributed to the betterment and prolongation of life? Those digital cadavers are, after all, composites of thousands of individual photographs of a real human body.

Through photography, ideas about the care and presentation of the body are disseminated and avidly consumed. Editors and advertisers show us how our bodies should be groomed, clothed or adorned, attempting to bring them into line with prevailing standards of taste and beauty. And the modern – or should we say, postmodern – art of advertising is inconceivable without photographic images of the body, crafted to sell not only body-care products and clothing but – through an alchemy of suggestion – any product in existence.

Mass-media entertainers like Madonna or Michael Jackson have used

photography to promote carefully engineered representations of androgyny or sexual and racial ambiguity. Politicians and ideologues of all persuasions have used photography to put forward visions of 'perfect' bodies as emblems of their own conceptions of a healthy body politic. Pornographers, too, have long understood the lure of sexually explicit photographs. But the same images are held up by feminists as proof of male domination and insensitivity. In and of itself, photography professes no morality, no allegiance.

Other areas are less contentious. Photographs record moments of athletic triumph and preserve the fleeting art of the dance. Educators rely heavily upon the medium to instruct students in a wide range of disciplines. War reporters find in photographs of broken bodies the most efficacious route to the emotional engagement of their readers. The police have long depended on photographic documentation as irrefutable evidence, while anthropologists have used the camera to measure and compare bodies in support of various theories of race, heredity and evolution (uses which cause contemporary anthropologists considerable anguish). Artists have relied upon photography as an aid to painting and sculpture or, more recently, as a creative medium in its own right. And parents the world over have trusted in the camera to record the growth of their offspring and commemorate their rites of passage. In short, where the human body is concerned, the powers of photography can be questioned, but never denied.

Andres Serrano
Aids Related Death 1992
From original colour transparency

INTRODUCTION

In the Autumn of 1879, a series of articles appeared in the *Photographic News*, an influential British journal, on a subject of great fascination to the Victorians – the Zulus of South Africa. These articles are remarkably revealing, not only of British perception of non-Western peoples, but of nineteenth-century attitudes generally to the human body. Directly or indirectly, they illuminate a whole range of issues highly significant for Victorian England: notions of race, concepts of beauty, sexuality and man's animal nature, beliefs about decency and morality and the distinction between 'savagery' and 'civilization', assumptions about social class, and even the rightful place of the body in art and science.

The image of the fierce Zulu warrior had taken firm hold on the British imagination because of the Zulu Wars of 1879. Vivid engraved prints depicting warriors in the heat of battle were widely popular. But the *Photographic News* was concerned with a different kind of Zulu image: photographic portraits. If these studies were stiff and lacklustre in comparison with the melodramatic prints, they had one feature that the public found quite mesmerizing – the unabashed and virtually total nakedness of the subjects.

Nakedness was something that people in the late nineteenth century found alternately fascinating and disturbing. Few opportunities existed for scrutinizing either the human body itself or an image of it. It was an age when dress was particularly restrictive and concealing and knowledge of another's body was mainly confined to the hands and face, which may explain the popularity at the time of the so-called sciences of phrenology and physiognomy which tried to 'read' into these physical features the inner constitution.

Anonymous
A Happy New Year (Zulu women) *c.* 1879
Modern print

What caught the attention of the *Photographic News* was the prosecution of a photographic dealer for displaying 'obscene photographs of semi-nude Zulus' in his windows. The Lord Mayor of London himself pronounced on 'the grossness and impropriety of Zulu fashions and sartorial customs'.[1] But the dealer argued that the subjects were merely depicted in their native dress, and the journal agreed, describing the photographs as 'ethnological studies' and therefore not only acceptable, but invaluable to science.

The authorities rightly suspected that the trade in Zulu imagery (and that of other tribal peoples), mostly depicting nubile young women, was not due entirely to dispassionate scientific curiosity or aesthetic expression. From photography's early days pornographers had found ways to hide behind 'the beautiful shield of photography' and newspapers and journals of the day were constantly reporting the confiscation of huge collections of sexually suggestive material on sale in shops. The *News* worried that the clampdown on the Zulu imagery was simply a pretext for 'a general raid upon photographers who were to be prosecuted for anything which could be construed as of questionable taste or decency'.[2]

The nudity of the Zulus was postulated as proof of primitive morality – the natural condition of savage races closer to nature and their animal ancestry. But it was one thing for the innocent 'natives' to 'dress' this way, another to put images of their bodies on display before the civilized world. Their nakedness was equated with ugliness and looseness of morals. Should a gentleman ever allow an image of his wife to be exhibited anywhere near 'portraitures of half-naked actresses and entirely naked Zulu women, he can have but little respect for himself, for her, or for his position'.[3]

Perhaps the single most revealing event of the time was the public display of a group of Zulus in the Brussels Zoo, next door, by inference, to other 'exotic' animals. A photographer was sent to document the scene, but his intentions were misunderstood and he was attacked by his subjects. Lucky to escape unharmed, but with his equipment in pieces, he resolved never again to try his hand at 'Zulugraphy', or in fact to take photographs 'of any specimen of a savage race'.[4]

We are tempted to dismiss such behaviour and attitudes as hypocritical, but this is to oversimplify. In the 1860s and 1870s, intelligent men and women were becoming deeply interested in the relation of human beings to animals and of different races to each other. In spite of all its prejudices and stereotypes, the nineteenth century did see the rise of a genuine interest in the diversity of mankind. The emergence of anthropology as a scientific discipline was more or less simultaneous with the invention of photography. This new discipline was conceived as a fact-gathering, classifactory natural science, and since photography was seen as the purveyor of absolute truth, it was inevitable that it should be used to provide objective records of a people and their culture, aiding in measurement, analysis and classification. Although the general theoretical framework was centred on social evolution, on the hierarchies this suggested, and on race, in practice this meant close scrutiny of the human body, since an understanding of the body was considered to be the key to an understanding of race and culture. What lent the enterprise urgency was the conviction that tribal peoples were doomed to extinction. Zulus were not alone in being turned into spectacle. Pygmies, Sioux, Ainu and many other racial groups were paraded photographically before Western eyes.

In the late 1860s T. H. Huxley and John Lamprey drew up systems of standard procedures for ethnological photography. The naked subject was to be posed standing and sitting, fully frontal or in profile. Huxley placed his subjects next to a clearly marked measuring rod; Lamprey's were positioned in front of a metrological grid of 2-inch squares made from string. Much work was produced following the latter method, such as M. V. Portman and W. Molesworth's eleven-volume survey of the Andaman Islanders in the 1890s.[5] Other systems were proposed as well, but common to all was the fundamentally racist idea that the 'lower orders' would prove to be physically inferior.

Other scientists also recognized the potential of photography. From the early 1850s on, professional medical and photographic journals suggested ways in which photography could be used to further research in anatomy, physiology, histology and pathology. Many of the pioneering physicians in these areas were themselves photographers.[6]

L. Haase, a Berlin photographer, was employed to record the orthopaedic patients of a Dr H. W. Berend in the early 1860s. His subjects stand squarely in front of plain backgrounds, naked only to the extent required to show their condition. There is no pictorial impulse here – no desire to compose a pleasing 'picture'. But in a number of images a sweep of fabric is included, reminding us of the conventional treatment of nudes in the period. Though the fabric was probably there to disguise the heavy metal stand which supported the patient during the lengthy exposure, it also betrays a certain hesitancy in accepting a purely clinical approach.

Other conventions were also difficult to dislodge in depictions of the sick through to the end of the century. Many early images of patients look like portraits of perfectly healthy people. Oriental carpets, painted backdrops or incongruous props obscure the fundamental purpose of the image.

No such confusion between science and art is apparent in the 1861 studies of a hermaphrodite made by the distinguished Parisian photographer Nadar. In a series of eight studies, both full-figure and in close-up, he depicts his subject's condition with frankness and clarity. Other French photographers made a major contribution to nineteenth-century medicine at the Salpêtrière hospital in Paris. There, from 1862, Professor Charcot, a specialist in pathological anatomy, used the camera not simply as a tool with specific and limited functions but as a way of perceiving a broader picture of disease and treatment – the therapeutic situation. Charcot seems to have grasped the fact that photographic seeing was less an equivalent to straightforward vision than to the mediated process of perception. Photographs were taken at each stage of the patient's disease and cure.

The year 1882 saw the installation of the photographer Albert Londe as head of the hospital's well-equipped photographic studio. Working closely with Paul Richer, doctor and anatomy professor, Londe brought to the photography of patients with nervous disorders a 'photochronographic' method which used up to twelve lenses to capture movements too rapid for the eye to see.

The neurologist Guillaume-Benjamin Duchenne is also worthy of mention in the context of early research. Duchenne undertook the analysis of facial expressions through the application of electrical currents to specific muscles, setting out to create a universally valid facial vocabulary. (His work is more fully discussed on p. 109.)

Army medical photographers also pushed frontiers forward. The English-born William Bell was chief photographer of the U.S. Army Medical Museum

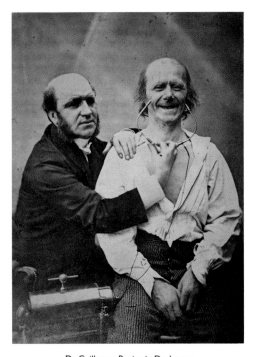

Dr Guillaume-Benjamin Duchenne
Dr Duchenne examining a subject in the course of his work on the analysis of facial expressions 1852-56
Albumen print

in the late 1860s. His clinical photographs of Civil War casualties, accompanied by detailed case histories, had a two-fold use: as teaching aids, and as evidence in future cases of disability compensation. Beginning in 1865, the museum published a seven-volume *Photographic Collection of the Surgical Section* which was to have a widespread effect on the education of physicians. Military authorities also found photography a useful tool in studying the impact on the body of carrying weapons and kit.

One of the most profound developments in medicine in the 1830s and 1840s had been the recognition of the cell as the fundamental living unit of the body. Photography would be used in this area to enormous advantage. Photomicrography allowed physicians to search for ever finer and more minute structures. A U.S. army surgeon, H. J. Woodward, used lantern slides made from his photomicrographs to demonstrate that cancer is a mutation of cells in the body and not the formation of new cells introduced from an outside source. **17**

Extravagant claims were made of photomicrography. Just as in the seventeenth century, when mechanistically minded observers 'saw' minute machine-like structures through the microscope, so certain photography enthusiasts 'saw' structures that they were predisposed to see. A particularly outlandish discovery was reported in the *Photographic News* in 1888 by George R. Rockwood of New York, under the rubric, 'a photo-physiological theory'[7]. Examining photomicrographs of brain tissue, he was astonished to find markings which seemed to him to be suspiciously like Chinese characters (note the lure of the exotic East!) or hieroglyphs. Amazed by this monumental find of 'pictures in the brain', Rockwood speculated that 'future literary executors shall be able to extract from the distinguished dead posthumous poems, suppressed opinions, the contents of "burned" letters, family secrets, or the mysteries of life that are buried.'[8]

Such a fanciful account reminds us of the extraordinary faith the nineteenth century put in science's capacity to unravel the mysteries of the human body, as well as the high expectations it had of photography. What many of the experimenters of the time seem to have shared was a desire to make visible the invisible. In this they were grappling with something tantalizingly close: only a few years later Wilhelm Konrad Röntgen would announce the equally fantastic but incontestably real X-ray. Pictures could now be made of the interior of living human bodies without opening them up. Röntgen's discovery would, like photography itself, contribute to the doctor's dependency on the visual sense rather than the sense of touch, on which physicians had relied for centuries.

In the mid-nineteenth century, the forces of law and order were busy with their own photographic enterprises. As early as 1841, criminals and suspicious persons in Paris were daguerreotyped and filed away for future reference. Soon after, the first photo-illustrated 'wanted' poster appeared in France. By mid-decade, every British criminal was being photographed, as was every murder victim and the scene of every crime. In the 1860s, some warders in British prisons were photographing all the prisoners in their charge and by 1870 this practice was mandatory in Great Britain.

In Europe and North America, too, photography was rapidly becoming 'one of the best safeguards against crime, seeing that none could escape its crucial observation'.[9] The Swiss authorities even required all vagrants to be photographed, on the principle that they would eventually gravitate toward crime. By 1872 the French were sufficiently persuaded of photography's usefulness to open the first true photographic service for the police. Among other advantages, photographs of scenes of crimes were found to be helpful in extracting confessions from suspects and were considered more trustworthy than the testimony of a witness.

It was in France, too, in 1882, that the first rigorous and precise method of recording a criminal's identity was developed. This forerunner of the modern police identity picture was devised by Alphonse Bertillon, chief of criminal investigation for the Paris police. It consisted of a photographic profile and frontal views, accompanied by measurements of the head, left fingers, left forearm and left foot, as well as body height. Bertillon took great pains with diffused lighting, the neutrality of his sitters' expressions, the distance from the lens, the angle of view, and so on. The presentation of the two finished prints (profile and frontal view) side by side was equally precise: each image had to be cut '0.01 m. above the hair'.[10] Bertillon knew that without standardization and precision comparisons would be meaningless, and identity could not be established with absolute certainty.

Dr Henry Clark
Inmate, West Riding Prison, Wakefield c. 1869
Albumen print

One of the fundamental passions of nineteenth-century science (soon to be shared by art) was that of movement. Scientists were searching for a unifying theory to explain diverse physical phenomena, and movement was postulated as being at the crux of the issue. Photography had a central role to play in this research. Eadweard Muybridge at the University of Pennsylvania, Etienne-Jules Marey at his 'Station Physiologique' in Paris, Albert Londe and Paul Richer at the Saltpetrière, even Duchenne in his studio making pictures of 'physionomie en mouvement' – here were the leading figures in the quest to penetrate to the heart of the matter by photographic means. For all their idiosyncratic approaches, they shared a distrust of the evidence of the senses and an appetite for the monumental. They were not the only, nor even the first photographers to tackle the problem – Nadar, for instance, had made earlier attempts to photograph rapid motion – but their work had a depth and intelligence which has sustained interest up to the present day.

Eadweard Muybridge's extensive oeuvre, published in *Animal Locomotion* (1887) and *The Human Figure in Motion* (1901), has always been recognized as a seminal achievement: 'The work should belong to every scientific and artistic institution in the world,' wrote the *Nation* on 19 January 1888, and scientists agreed. *Animal Locomotion* comprised 781 plates. Of these, 523 were on the subject of the human figure: men, women and children, normal and abnormal, naked and clothed, exerting one set of muscles or another in the exercise of a task. The stop-action photographs, with between twelve and fifty on a single plate, depicted hundreds of actions – some simple, such as sitting, walking or throwing; others more complex, such as 'drinking from a goblet while standing' or 'one woman disrobing another'. Curiously, one sees in this last image, and in certain others, the impassive visage of science giving way, and notions of art and morality creep in – a woman covers her face in shame at her sudden state of nakedness, for example. Muybridge did have problems convincing many of his models to undress and men seemed to find the idea more threatening than women. He reported that his greatest difficulty was 'in inducing mechanics to go through the motions of their trade in a nude condition'.[11]

Etienne-Jules Marey was Muybridge's colleague and rival. 'The prime cause of movement in the living being seems to be of a special order, without parallel in inanimate bodies', he wrote early in his career, 'but once movement is produced it is the same whatever its source.'[12] It would be fair to say that this great French investigator was more interested in physiology than morphology. Particularly wary of the evidence of hand and eye, he put his trust in instruments that could measure precisely 'amplitude, force, duration, regularity and shape'.[13] Photography took its place alongside other instruments and soon proved extremely efficacious in, as the philosopher François Dagognet has put it, 'capturing and translating phenomena in a web of inscription, where it first became visible, and then readable (that is, intelligible) . . . , Marey thereby hoped to attain his goal: 'the language of nature'.[14]

Muybridge and Marey, though certainly the towering figures in the study of the human body in motion, were followed by others. The Prussian photographer Otto Anschutz made use of Muybridge's method to win acclaim for his highly accomplished serial imagery of athletes and gymnasts in the 1880s, and the French photographer Charles Fremont used Marey's Station Physiologique to photograph the movements of manual workers.

Constant reference is made in nineteenth-century writing on photography to the medium's extraordinary clarity of detail, its 'microscopic fidelity to nature'.[15] The word 'microscopic' suggests a sense of revelation, as if no one had ever before looked at the physical world anywhere near as closely. This attribute was of particular appeal to artists interested in the human body.

In his 1986 study of nineteenth-century French photography of the body, André Rouillé makes a useful distinction between the portrait and the nude, between subject and object.[16] In a portrait, the specific body (the person) being pictured is the subject; he or she has initiated the transaction, and the photographer is merely the facilitator. In the nude, the transaction is reversed; the photographer initiates the event; the body is depersonalized, the object. Like the medical, police or anthropological photograph, the artistic nude is an image made by and for the perusal of others.

When the daguerreotype was invented in 1839 it had an immediate appeal for artists. Sir John Herschel reported to William Henry Fox Talbot that it gave 'a richness and delicacy of execution' which surpassed the finest engraving, and set 'all painting at an immeasurable distance'.[17] But daguerreotypes were one-of-a-kind and expensive, and therefore out of the reach of all but the wealthiest of artists. Not until the introduction of the glass negative in 1851, coupled with the albumen print, would the production of nudes specifically for artists be commercially feasible.

Painters, sculptors, graphic artists and others who could not afford daguerreotypes often could not afford models either; photographic prints gave them what they needed in the way of poses, and something more – the time to scrutinize the body in any specific pose, returning to it as often as necessary. The required poses were chosen from catalogues, and, towards the end of the century, when the practice was well-established, from specialist magazines.[18]

The treatment of the body in these 'studies from nature' was of two types. Either the nudes were stripped of all decoration, with the emphasis solely on the body, or the body was part of a decorative scheme which involved flowing draperies, oriental rugs, musical instruments, armour and the like. Either way, the body was posed according to the conventions of fine art, notably those of antiquity or orientalism: the nude female supine on a couch, arranged so as to maximize the curve of breast and thigh; the eyes closed or averted, feigning abandon or sleep; the rich, billowing fabric hinting at pleasures of the boudoir. In the more ambitious schemes mirrors were sometimes employed to give simultaneous views of different facets of the body. Specific styles of painting were often imitated, even specific paintings – Ingres held particular appeal, as did the seventeenth-century Dutch school.

Many artists seem to have made use of such studies. Some took their own, others commissioned them. Some used them privately while denying the practice publicly, afraid of being accused of reliance on a lowly mechanical instrument; others used them but avoided comment on the issue; a few, Eugène Delacroix included, proclaimed their enthusiasm. A general complaint was that 'woman' – the generalized, idealized being – was a purely artistic creation, and that the woman revealed by photography was specific, identifiable and flawed.

The nude photograph also caused anxiety among female models. They too were accustomed to the idealizing vision of the fine arts and did not relish the camera's fidelity to nature. Moreover, they worried that, whereas an artist rarely allowed a sketch to go out of his possession, a photographer might inadvertently or not let slip an extra print which would surface as erotica. Models tended to be working-class women, such as domestic servants, who were attracted to the relatively high pay, but they sometimes included middle-class acquaintances or relatives of the photographer. For all such women, the consequences of images straying out of the photographer's control could be devastating.

Photography of the female nude can be seen in the context of art history dating back to the Renaissance, but for the male nude precedents from classical antiquity would prove to be a far greater inspiration. This was especially so for photographers caught up in the new passion for body-building or physical culture. Eugene Sandow in England and the United States and Edmond Desbonnet in France reached out to their potential clients with the help of promotional photography. Photographic imagery of their own magnificent bodies was held up as proof of the efficacy of their methods.

The relatively unmediated realism that appealed to the artist also excited pornographers. The earliest erotic nudes were daguerreotypes, often hand-tinted with loving attention to the flesh. The subjects were young and female, the preferred mode of viewing was stereo, the clients were men of means, and the authors were generally anonymous. The uniqueness of each daguerreotype meant that production was never more than a cottage industry. In Paris, centre of the trade, the less explicit imagery was made available through opticians and the more explicit through the luxury brothels. With the introduction of the print, the scale of the enterprise changed dramatically and by 1865 photographs were available at 'print sellers and fancy stationers', though it was still illegal to send them through the mail.[19]

For much of the nineteenth century, photography of the nude was confined to its role as handmaiden to the fine arts. Towards the end of the century, however, increasing numbers of photographers argued for photography's legitimacy as an art in its own right. For these advocates, the photographic nude was not a means to an end, but an end in itself. Ironically, these Pictorialists, or Impressionist photographers as they were sometimes called, felt they had to prove their case by rejecting the photograph's essential attribute: its descriptive clarity and literalness – the very aspect that had attracted artists in the first place – and substituting for it painterly effects, such that the works could be confused with charcoal or pastel drawings, aquatints or engravings.

So the 'microscopic attention to detail' became anathema; detail was to be suppressed through soft-focus or handworked effects. Backgrounds were to be

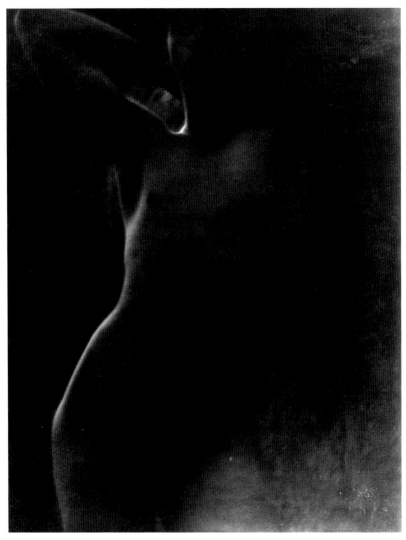

Frederick Holland Day
Nude in Shadow 1910
Gelatin silver print

painted out, roughly textured papers substituted for the 'commercial' albumen, and myth and legend invoked in the Symbolist vein. 'Telling a story, preferably a moral one', notes Jorge Lewinski in his study of the nude, 'and thereby creating a narrative image was another way in which nineteenth- and early **24** twentieth-century photographers tried to overcome the mundane literalness of photography.'[20] Too mundane also was the physical world of the here-and-now; there is little trace of the gritty nineteenth-century urban and industrial environment in a Pictorialist photograph. Clothes were happily discarded, as too-precise signifiers of time and place. Nakedness was equated with innocence and proximity to nature. The bodies depicted were inevitably young and female, though pre-pubescent boys were acceptable, as were older women, provided they represented motherhood. The mood was languor; the models' demeanour expressed modesty and passivity.

To modern eyes, Pictorialist imagery appears at best sentimental and at worst kitsch. But there can be no doubt that the collective efforts of its practitioners created a climate of respect for photography as a bona fide art form and an enthusiasm in the public domain which would serve it well in the following century.

Social and cultural historians generally acknowledge that the nineteenth century 'ended' with the First World War. They have not always agreed on the precise effects of the conflict on attitudes to the body, but there is widespread consensus as to the magnitude of its impact. Ten million bodies obliterated, many millions more maimed and traumatized – these were the brute facts with which each individual had to contend. For those who survived – and even for those who had lived through the war years far from the field of battle – the deprivations suffered by the body led to a new awareness of its essence and of the extent of its vulnerability in the face of a highly technological world. In retrospect, some of these changes seem to have been for the better – for example, there were certainly forces which contributed to the liberation of women – but equally there were forces which created anxieties and conflicts which to this day have not been satisfactorily resolved.

How, then, did postwar photography deal with this much-abused body? In *The Rites of Spring*, cultural historian Modris Ekstein cites various reports from the decade following the war which argued that photography had proved an inadequate means of conveying the magnitude of the horrors. War photographers blamed the censors; the American James Hare grumbled that 'to so much as make a snapshot without official permission in writing means arrest'.[21] But in a prescient article in 1928, Erich Maria Remarque, future author of the hugely popular war novel *All Quiet on the Western Front* took photography itself to task for fragmenting the world into neatly formatted rectangles which ripped events out of context and created false pictures of reality.[22] Nevertheless, though photography painted only a piecemeal picture of the war's true damage, the volume of photographs printed in the press had the effect of bringing home to the public the scale of the carnage.

From the twenties on, normal, healthy bodies depicted in the new photographically illustrated mass-circulation magazines in Europe, Asia and North America were more naturalistically and realistically portrayed than ever before in history. The venerable studio portrait, with its stiffly posed, invariably seated figure looked increasingly anachronistic in the face of this spontaneous genre, whereby people from all walks of life were depicted candidly and unselfconsciously pursuing their daily lives. Gestures and other expressive aspects of body language could be 'caught' by the new cameramen, armed with tiny portable cameras and fast film. The rapidly expanding public for these magazines was captivated by the new style of imagery. Some contemporary observers detected a new body language, a shift in the way people walked and expressed themselves physically. If this was indeed the case, photography may have been partly responsible. Just how viscerally the public felt these images is evident in this 1926 description by the social critic Kurt Tucholsky: ' . . . a photograph if properly chosen punches, boxes, whistles, grips the heart and conveys the only truth.'[23]

Conditions of war had allowed women to adopt far less restrictive garments, and, as hemlines rose, ankles and feet appeared. Cosmetics no longer signified loose morals, and rouge, lipstick and eye-shadow were increasingly in demand. This 'new' female body was presented in its most idealized form in the pages of the fashion magazines *Vogue* and *Harper's Bazaar*. *Vogue* had introduced what we now think of as fashion photography in the second decade of the century, notably in the form of Baron Adolf de Meyer's dreamy soft-focus apparitions, but this style was rejected after the war in favour of a bold crisp modernism which promoted the more boyish flapper over more matronly ideals: shorter skirts, smaller hats, and smaller hips and breasts became more desirable. In the best imagery of Edward Steichen and George Hoyningen-Huene, both in turn chief photographers for *Vogue*, the female body was made to conform to schemes of high art, whether avant-garde styles like Cubism and Constructivism, or more traditional forms derived from classical antiquity and the Neoclassicism of David or Ingres. But eventually the public appetite for spontaneous and informal depictions of bodies had its impact. It was no coincidence that the first of the great 'realist' fashion photographers, Martin Munkacsi, had started out as a photojournalist of the new school. From 1934 on, the two modes of depicting bodies would co-exist comfortably on the fashion spreads.

And what of art photography and the body in the postwar years? 'Body' still meant female, but a new breed of women emerged. Gone was the dreamy Symbolism of mist-shrouded nudes and idyllic moonlit haunts. Real flesh-and-blood bodies were brought into sharp focus. Even photographers who had practised the old style in the years preceding the conflict knew that things had changed. Edward Steichen, for example, prewar Impressionist par excellence, moved in his treatment of the nude to a bold new modernist style which dispensed with Pictorialist effects and began to see the body in an essentially sculptural fashion, as if flesh were just one of the new materials of the age, like concrete, glass and steel.

A far different approach was taken by Steichen's mentor, Alfred Stieglitz. For twenty years, beginning in 1917, this uncompromising advocate of photography as art, who must be credited with aspects of a modernist vision well before the war, photographed the painter Georgia O'Keeffe in the nude. Ignoring standard conventions – of both painting and pictorial photography – Stieglitz used his camera to explore lovingly every nuance of O'Keeffe's body. Taking his cue from Picasso's and Kandinsky's theories of painting, he understood that photography was not merely an objective record of a physical reality but a mirror, or equivalent, of the imagemaker's own emotional state. On the West Coast, Imogen Cunningham and Edward Weston likewise abandoned myth and allegory and enthusiastically explored the body as a subject in itself. If the full-figure nude was by now a well-established tradition in photography, the body could be coaxed to reveal another dimension of itself through fragmentation. Cameras moved in closely to the body, playing a game of geometry and abstraction.

For European photographers and artists Realism was an attractive option. Brassaï's famous informal studies of Parisian prostitutes and Raoul Hausmann's **27** imagery of naked bodies on a beach demonstrated a willingness to face facts about the body which were by no means flattering. Hausmann's bodies (which included his own) are seen from unorthodox angles and vantage points. They reject all coyness and prettification and stress instead a raw, earthy physicality. There is nothing of Steichen's or Weston's elegant stone-textured skin, Cunningham's sensual geometry, or Stieglitz's passion. Hausmann argued:

> What is important is that our optical awareness rids itself of classical notions of beauty and opens itself more and more to the beauty of the instant and of those surprising points of view that appear for a brief moment and never return; those are what make photography an art.[24]

But European sensibilities were generally more attuned to paradox and mystery than their North American counterparts. The American-born Man Ray, for instance, found a more supportive environment for his fertile imagination in Paris, where he transformed the naked female body through solarization, negative printing and the like, creating an oeuvre suffused with mystery, wit and eroticism. Like Hausmann, Man Ray argued that photography *could* be art, but only if the eye were subordinated to the imaginative faculties, to an inner vision.

In the hands of French, German, Polish, Czechoslovakian, Hungarian and other European photographers the body was subjected to infinite trans-formations and transfigurations through reflection and refraction, solarization, multiple exposure, a deliberate confusion with mannequins and dolls, photo-montage and collage, multiple exposure, and a variety of idiosyncratic printing techniques – 'a new continent of optical poetry', the Czech experimenter Karel Teige called it.[25] There was a disturbing note of misogyny in many of these often tortured visions, though it only infrequently achieved the level of mania that is apparent in the savagely dismembered dolls of Hans Bellmer.

The body features heavily in Surrealist and Constructivist montage and collage throughout Europe. Disembodied eyes and hands were motifs which occur again and again in the work of artists such as Teige in Czechoslovakia, Alexander Rodchenko in Russia and Kazimierz Podsadecki in Poland. Sometimes the message was metaphysical, at other times social or political. Together these works convey a sense of a world which has slipped its moral and spiritual moorings, and hint at deep and unresolved psychological distress.

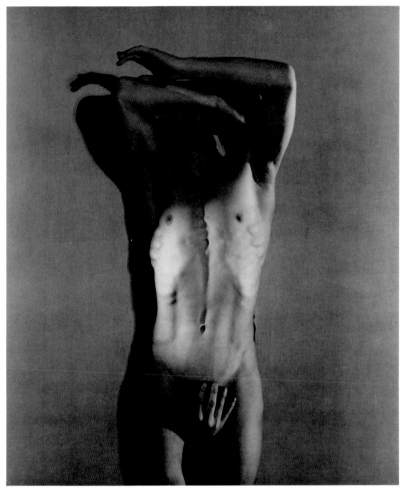

George Platt Lynes
Untitled 1936
Gelatin silver print

The Second World War could only heighten these anxieties. Afterwards, photography would continue to extend and refine the new vocabulary of photographic expression but what was lost was the prewar faith, fervently expressed by many photographers, that an impassioned photographic vision could actually transform social and political reality. This fervent hope, notes photographic historian Christopher Phillips, would ' . . . disappear almost entirely; instead a sophisticated photographic language was used by **29** photographers like [Harry] Callahan or Ray Metzker to give form to the ever more elusive concerns of a meditative sensibility . . . a reaffirmation of inner experience and the exercise of individual creativity'.[26] In this light, witness for example Bill Brandt's Henry Moore-like fragments of the body, Ralph Gibson's elegant formalism of truncated shapes, Holly Wright's thick male torsos contrived from puny fingers and thumbs, or the way in which Arno Rafael Minkkinen weaves himself seamlessly into the Finnish landscape.

The motives, strategies and approaches undertaken by photographers are as infinitely varied as the human bodies depicted. Whether they have chosen to focus on their own bodies or the bodies of models, friends or lovers; whether they have approached their subject with an unflinching documentary realism, or a passion for abstraction and design, or with the need to transform the body into some other animate or inanimate being, landscape, or fantasy . . . whether their motives have been scientific, aesthetic or political, photographers continue to find in the human body a subject of infinite potential.

Dr M. Aszal Ansary
An 8-week human foetus rests in an adult's palm 1991
Gelatin silver print

A Guide to the Chapters

The photographs have been arranged according to a framework of twelve chapters, the contents of which are as follows:

FRAGMENTS: the body 'in part'

FIGURES: the tradition of the full-figure nude

PROBES: the realm of scientific exploration

FLESH: the vulnerable, mortal body; an emphasis on corporeality

PROWESS: the body at its peak of physical condition; dance and sports

EROS: the body as an object of sexual desire

ESTRANGEMENT: the oppressed and victimized body

IDOLS: the idealized body

MIRROR: the camera turned on the photographer's own body

POLITIC: the body as a site of contested meaning and value

METAMORPHOSIS: the body transformed

MIND: the body in the realm of dream, fantasy and obsession

Any single image has diverse attributes; what these attributes are depends as much on what the viewer reads into them as what the photographer intended; one viewer sees beauty where another sees ugliness; one sees an object of desire where another sees sexual exploitation; one sees scientific data where another sees an unintended aesthetic effect. By including an image in a particular chapter I mean to focus on one significant attribute of the image, one possible reading. However, the chapters are not seen as mutually exclusive, and other possible readings are not denied. Indeed, the inclusion of one photographer's imagery in several chapters is a tribute to a multifaceted vision.

FRAGMENTS

I'm interested in producing truncated shapes in proportion to the frame and composition, shapes that are preferably luminous. I'm not interested in the full-figure; I want to abstract forms.

RALPH GIBSON, *Nude: Theory*, 1979

Photographic fragmentation of the human body, at least in terms of a bonafide aesthetic practice, is essentially a twentieth-century phenomenon. The nineteenth-century maker of a nude was predominantly concerned with fabricating academic-style full-figure studies which could be used as aids by painters and sculptors. And although occasionally he would be expected also to provide separate images of hands and feet, these were meant to show greater anatomical detail and were never intended as works of art in their own right.

That is not to say that there are no nineteenth-century precedents to twentieth-century 'fragments', but they are found in other contexts. There is, for example, André Disdéri's 1860s mosaic image showing the feet of the dancers at the Paris Opéra (36), or Louis Pierson's famous portrait of the Countess Castiglione in which she holds an oval picture frame to her eye in a play on exposure and concealment. There is a marvellous 1853 study of Madame Hugo's hand by Auguste Vacquerie as well, and no doubt other such treasures exist. But these are hardly fragments of the body in the fully modern sense – they reveal no secret regions normally concealed beneath the clothing and the parts depicted are presented as emblems of personality, social standing or occupation.

Such photographs fall clearly within the context of portraiture rather than the nude. In the nineteenth century, the fragment as we conceive it today would have been unthinkable. First of all, photography of the naked body unsettled Victorians whenever it was encountered outside the realms of high art and pure

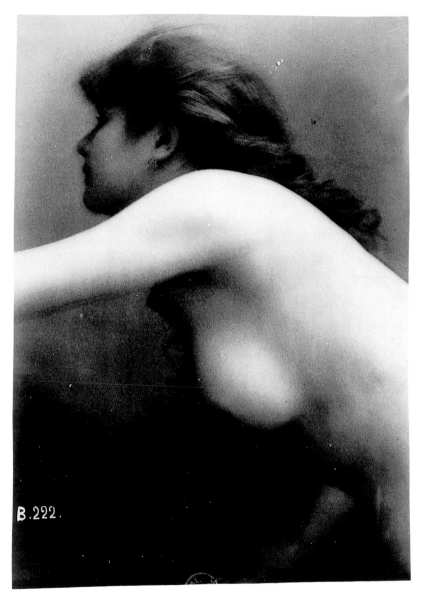

B.222.

L. Bonnard
Untitled c. 1880
Albumen print

science. Fragmenting the body would have seemed positively 'indecent', to use a word much employed by critics of the period. Moreover, it hardly even occurred to photographers that there was any aesthetic potential in a fragmentary vision – they were completely absorbed in working out an aesthetic of the figure.

So photography of the time only hints at the potential for the aesthetically autonomous fragment. We see such precedents in a beautiful 1851 calotype image of a hand by the painter/photographer Charles Nègre and in a profile of the upper part of a woman's body by L. Bonnard from later in the century (33). There is also an anonymous, enigmatic American tintype from the 1860s which suggests some meaningful personal commemoration, or possibly betrays a yearning to bridge the chasm between generations (37). But it is fair to say that, these few pictures aside, there were no conscious, sustained artistic efforts to depict or comprehend the body in terms of the fragment before the early decades of the twentieth century.

What then paved the way for the twentieth-century photographer's obsession with the fragment? Possibly one factor was the widespread practice, beginning in the 1870s, of 'instantaneous photography'. Amateurs and professionals alike delighted in the unintended effects which resulted from odd angles, blurs, distortions of foreground objects, unexpected cropping or the 'cutting-off' of figures as they suddenly moved into or out of the frame. These motifs found their way into the paintings of Degas and others, and became a standard feature of family albums, as the appeal of the stiff, thoroughly conventionalized studio portrait receded. 'By the power of convincing images', notes photohistorian Aaron Scharf, 'photography served, in these and in other respects, to undermine any ideas of an immutable perception of nature.'[1]

Certainly the scientific propensity to slice up time and space into ever finer units contributed generally to a new consciousness about the natural world, and wore away the belief that the evidence of the senses provided all that was required. The revelations of scientist/photographers like Duchenne, Marey and Muybridge had a marked impact on avant-garde artists. Cubists and Futurists in turn influenced photographers interested in aesthetics. Close-ups, which were being employed to stunning effect in the cinema, must also have been an influential factor.

Medical photographs too may have contributed to the shift towards a more fragmentary vision of the body. Nineteenth-century anatomy witnessed what Tracy Teslow calls 'the triumph of the fragment'.[2] Lithography and refined colour printing techniques enabled anatomists to reveal the secrets of the body with ever increasing accuracy and precision, and photography and X-ray technology were seen as excellent tools. Notes Teslow: 'Increasingly images of the body presented fragments. Bits of human flesh were objectified, quantified, codified, rationalized and thus existed apart from the whole to which they belonged.'[3] By the 1920s photographers of the nude had accepted the fragment as a viable option.

Since then, many photographers have chosen to focus on the fragment. We think of the rigorous 'New Objectivity' of German photographers of the 1920s

Alfred Stieglitz
Untitled (Hands of Helen Freeman) c. 1918
Toned silver gelatin print

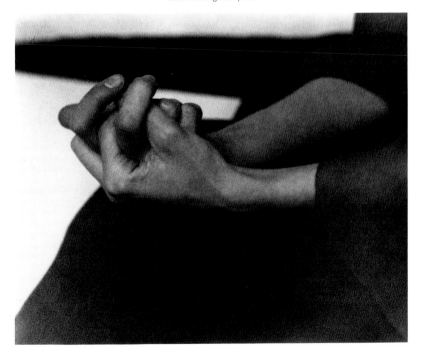

André Adolphe Eugène Disdéri
Les Jambes de l'Opéra (Legs at the Opéra) c. 1864
Albumen *carte-de-visite*

and 1930s, practitioners like August Sander and Max Burchartz, or the *F64* group in California, notably Edward Weston and Imogen Cunningham. But we find effective body fragmentation everywhere – in twentieth-century dance photography, in the appropriation of body parts in Surrealist and Constructivist photography and collage, in war photography and within the tradition of the nude. The sense of dislocation implicit in a fragmentary vision is in itself an evocative metaphor for the modern condition.

Some photographers limit themselves to the torso, stripping the body of its head and limbs just up to the point where the integrity of the whole is threatened. David Buckland, for example, focuses on the torso of a dancer, compressing her tightly into his 'box' of a frame (50). Many proponents of fragmentation have remarked on this need to crop off the head, or at least the face, which is otherwise too compelling – and distracting – a focus. This marks an interesting reversal of the nineteenth-century practice where the head was the central interest, said to be 'the ruling part of the figure', as if it lived independently of it – literally 'above' it – the sanctuary of morality, mind and spirit. Perhaps it was in reaction to this that modern photographers took the radical step of banishing the head entirely from their compositions.

The eye, however, is another matter. With the exception of the hand, which is invested with almost magical associations of character and personal identity, it is the most photographed of all bodily components. That hand and eye enjoy a privileged status among photographers is not surprising; they are, after all, at the root of the art and craft of photography.

Anonymous
Untitled c. 1860s
Tintype

37

Robert Mapplethorpe
Milton Moore 1981
Gelatin silver print

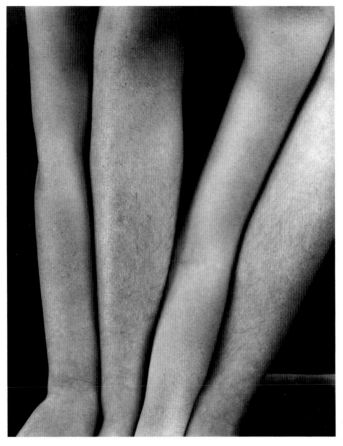

Edward Weston
Nude, Charis, Arms and Legs 1934
Gelatin silver print

At first glance, twentieth-century fragments appear to fall into three general categories. In the first we find the Realist fragment, where a portion of the body is subjected to intense scrutiny. Emphasis is on objective clarity. The German photographer August Sander worked from the 1920s through the 1950s on a series of just such clinically precise pictures, depicting body parts – or what he called, as only a photographer of the machine age could, 'Man's organic tools'.[4] The close-ups of Robert Davies, a young British photographer, might be seen as extending this tradition (48, 49).

39

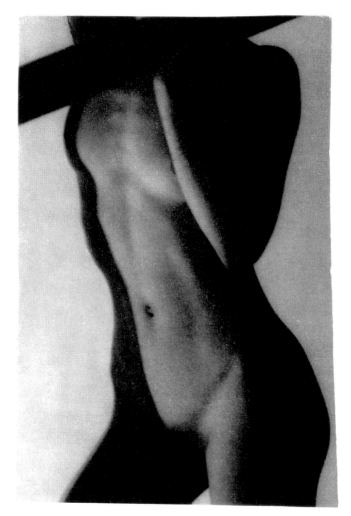

František Drtikol
Nude with Shadow 1945
Gelatin silver print

(right) Ernestine Ruben
Peek A Boo Fingers 1987
Gelatin silver print

In the second, the formalist fragment, the emphasis is on outline, shape, volume, abstraction, design – a geometry is constructed from the raw material of the body. The Czechoslovakian photographer František Drtikol's *Nude with* **40** *Shadow* of 1945 (*above*) is a prime example. Details of flesh and hair are

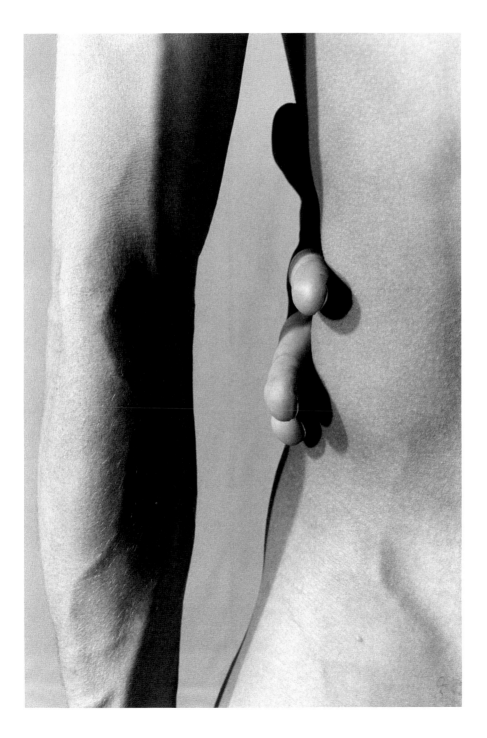

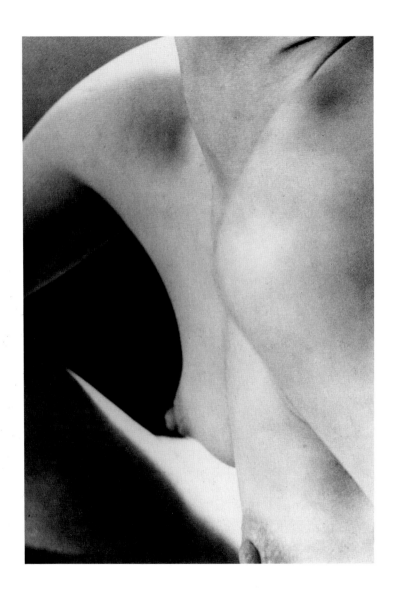

Umbo
Nude 1930
Gelatin silver print

Imogen Cunningham
Nude 2 1939
Gelatin silver print

suppressed in favour of rhythm and harmonious form. No scars or growths are allowed to impinge on the smooth, seamless textures of skin. At the root of these formalist abstractions, it seems, is a yearning for an idealized, immortal body.

The third category we might call the transformative or perhaps ambiguous fragment. Here we find attempts to transcend literal interpretations in order to

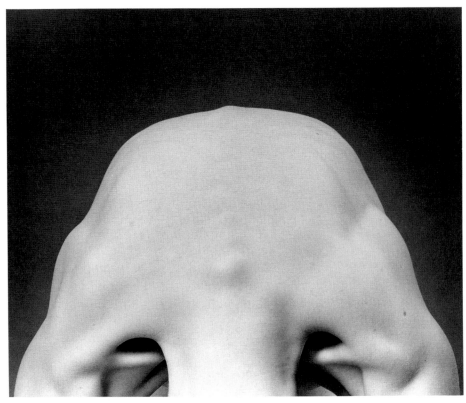

Pierre Radisic
Sonja 1987
Gelatin silver print

evoke some other order of being, animate or inanimate. It takes a moment to decipher such pictures, to realize that the 'skull' presented by Belgian photographer Pierre Radisic is in fact a woman's back, the 'eye-sockets' of the skull no more than a mirage formed by the configuration of arms and neck (*above*). Or that the two inquisitive rodents peering at each other in Tono Stano's *Private Performance II* (58) are in reality human feet, distant relations, perhaps, to the snaking foot mesmerized by the light in Bill Brandt's *Nude, Belgravia* (53). Or to work out what strange species of humanity people the dreamworld of Ernestine Ruben (41, and *right*).

Ernestine Ruben
Brooklyn Bridge 1987
Gelatin silver print

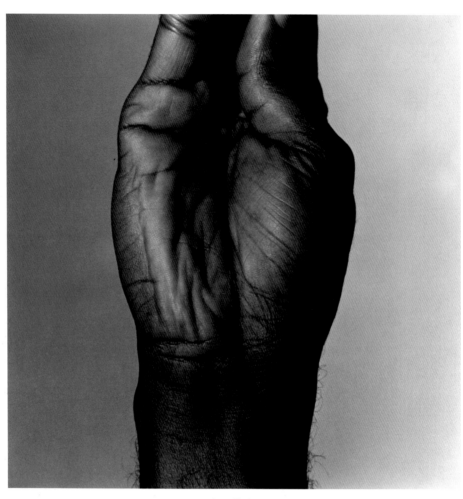

Lynn Davis
Black Hand, New York City 1978
Gelatin silver print

In fairness to the photographers, however, these discrete categories hardly do justice to the complexity of their ideas. Lynn Davis's monumental hand (*above*), for example, is quintessentially realist, down to the precisely rendered individual hairs on the wrist and the minute creases in the skin. Yet this is hardly a clinical treatment in the Sander manner. Instead she invests this magnificent object with an aura of dignity and independent pride.

46

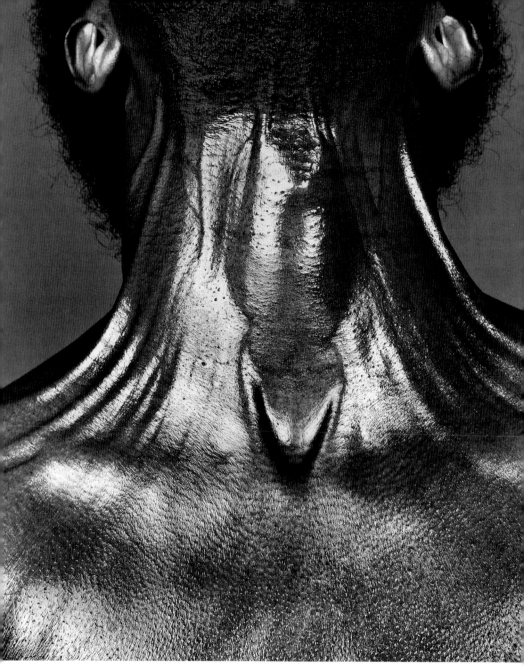

Pierre Radisic
Lucky 1983
Gelatin silver print

In the close-ups of Robert Davies (*above* and *right*) there is also something more than objective description. Revelation comes from seeing the body so closely, magnified (in the original prints) seventeen or eighteen times. It is as if we were holding a high-powered magnifying glass to a part of the body, or searching our faces in the mirror for a tell-tale wrinkle or blemish. The strength of this literalist approach is in its directness and honesty. Prettifying elements of 'composition' and 'form' hold little meaning. We are attracted or repelled by the raw physical facts. A tuft of hair in an ear or tiny unruly hairs on the head strike us – to our surprise – as profoundly beautiful, hinting at other natural forms.

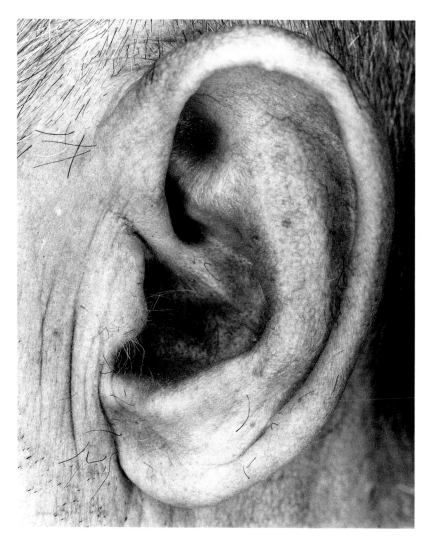

(opposite) **Robert Davies**
Eye 1 1992
Gelatin silver print

Robert Davies
Ear 1 1992
Gelatin silver print

49

The self-portraiture of John Coplans should also caution us against simplistic notions of 'type' where fragments are concerned (*right*, 57, 59). These works are formally complex and highly realistic, yet they still manage to convey a sense of transformation and mystery, of the body as a fortress (with fists poised to do battle in its defence) or as an archaic mammal. Coplans himself professes no documentary interest in his own body, no fascination with self. His body is as any other, specified only by age and gender. 'My photographs', he writes, 'recall the memories of the human race.'[5] □

(below) David Buckland
Torso III 1979
Platinum print

(right) John Coplans
Self-portrait 1984
Gelatin silver print

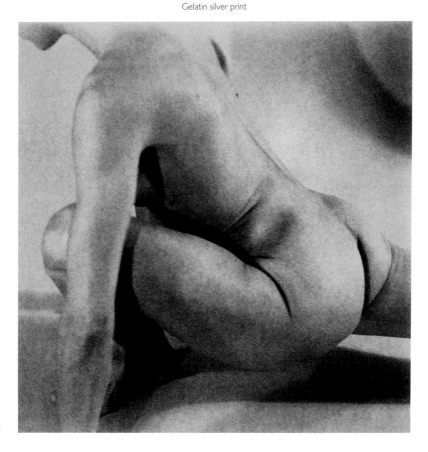

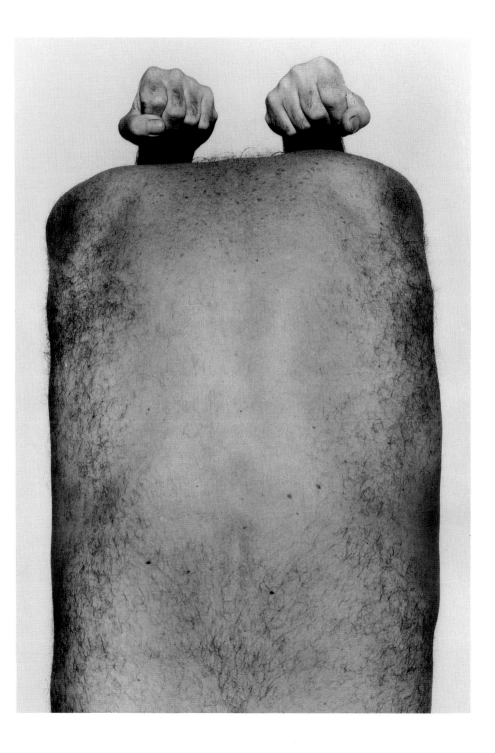

Tono Stano
Man in a Frame 1991
Gelatin silver print

Bill Brandt
Nude, Belgravia 1951
Gelatin silver print

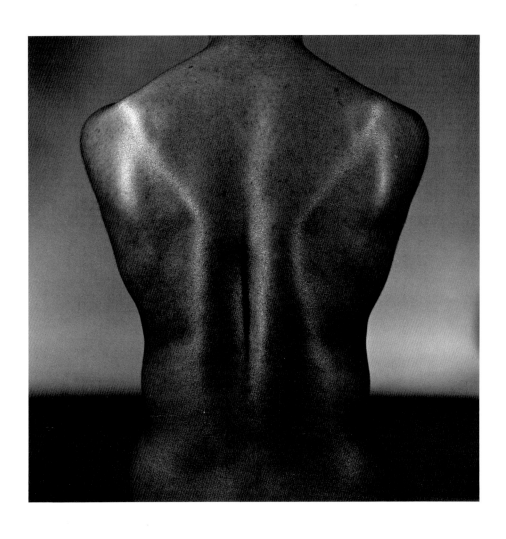

Lynn Davis
Black Back, New York City 1978
Gelatin silver print

Edward Weston
Nude 1939
Gelatin silver print

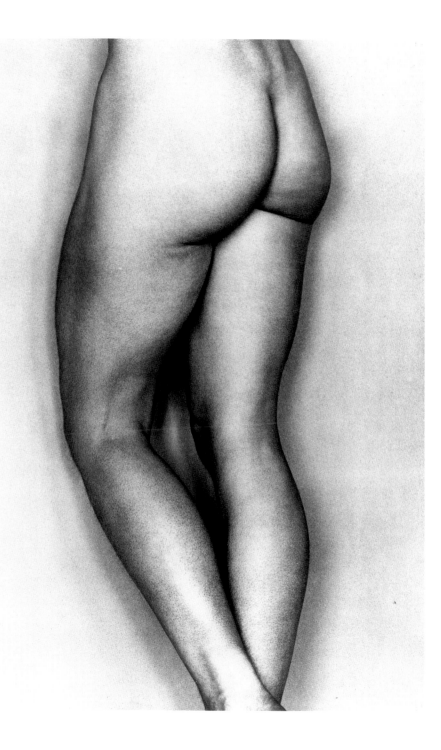

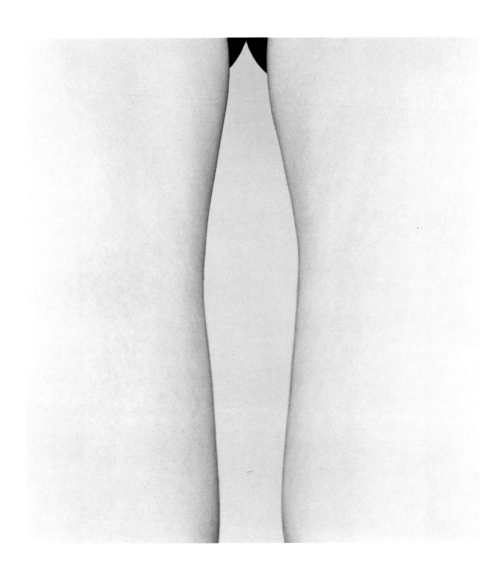

Pierre Radisic
Veronica 1986
Gelatin silver print

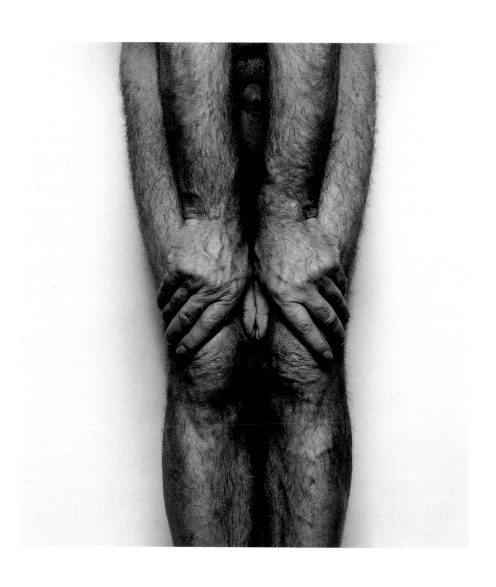

John Coplans
Self-portrait 1985
Gelatin silver print

57

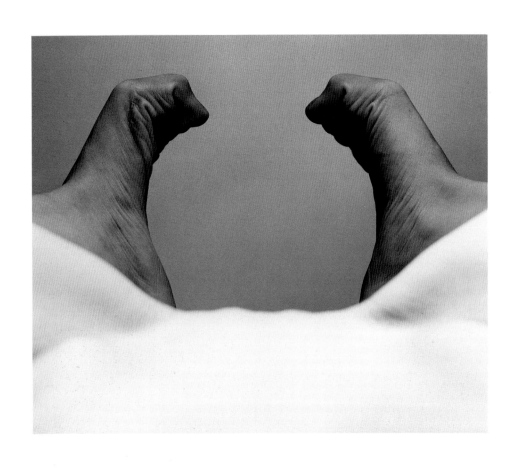

Tono Stano
Private Performance II 1991
Gelatin silver print

John Coplans
Self-portrait 1984
Gelatin silver print

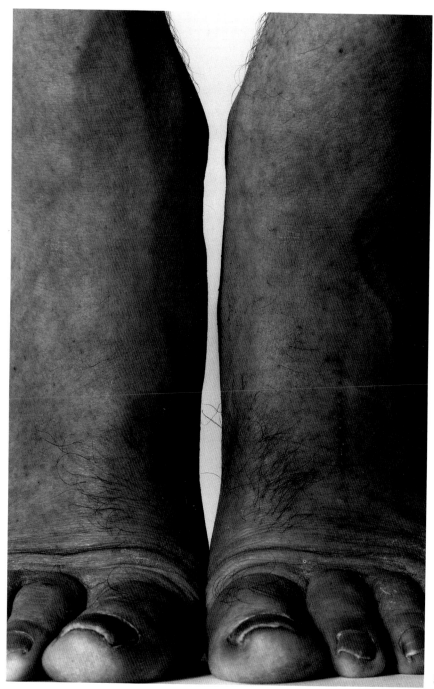

FIGURES

The photographer has an immense advantage over the painter by reason of his being able to obtain a view of the entire figure at once upon the focusing plate.

The Photographic News, 20 January 1865

When the body is mentioned in the context of photography, what usually springs to mind is the nude, which has established itself as a venerable tradition over the past one hundred years. For most of the nineteenth century, however, the situation was different on two counts. Firstly, the word 'body', with all its fleshly associations, was seldom used in discussions on photography: nudes were commonly referred to as 'figures'.

The early years of photography corresponded to a period of excessive prudery, when both men and women began to conceal their bodies with increasing thoroughness. As cultural historian Stephen Kern notes, 'Those Victorians who dominated public morality came to regard their bodies as a threat to respectability, and their attitude toward them was a combination of denial, distortion and fear.'[1] This campaign of denial was particularly harsh on the bodies of women, who for much of the nineteenth century wore constricting clothing which actually deformed the body and impaired its physiological functions.

Secondly, and not surprisingly in this climate of opinion, the photographic nude was not seen as a promising avenue to explore. The nude was established as the province of the painter and sculptor; in fact, mastery of the nude was at the core of the highly structured 'academic' system of training for artists.

However, although Victorians were willing to accept idealized nude figures depicted on canvas and sculpted in marble, they took offence at the fact that a photograph showed a real, identifiable human being. It was one thing

Oscar Gustave Rejlander
The Infant Photography Giving the Painter an Additional Brush 1856
Albumen print

for an 'amoral lithograph' to spring from an artist's imagination, but quite another to require a real woman to pose nude.[2] If photography was to have a role to play, considered opinion maintained that it should be that of handmaiden to the fine arts, a function acknowledged pictorially by the eminent Victorian painter-turned-photographer Oscar Gustave Rejlander in his 1856 image *The Infant Photography Giving the Painter an Additional Brush* (*above*).

What happened in private, however, was another matter. In a cultural climate where women's bodies were so hidden that a glimpse of an ankle could be sexually arousing, it is not surprising that daguerreotypes were immediately commandeered for the purposes of erotic gratification. And since eroticism is about fantasy, it was only natural that photographers would contrive exotic settings and pose their models languorously in the manner of well-known paintings.[3] Occasionally, however, we find a daguerreotype nude which hints at **61** a loving relationship between photographer and model (82), suggesting that early on certain photographers recognized the medium as an intensely personal one. However, as such daguerreotypes are inevitably anonymous (which was the best way for the photographer to stay out of trouble), we shall never be sure of their makers' intentions.

We can be fairly certain, though, that the 1843 French daguerreotype of a male nude on page 65 was made for a sculptor or painter. The relaxed, confident pose of the model suggests that he knew that the image would remain a private affair; possibly the model is the artist himself, curious to see his own body objectively.

Many nineteenth-century artists would utilize such photographs as aids, though few could afford the more expensive, one-of-a-kind daguerreotypes. Artists recognized that such photographic studies saved time and avoided the expense of a model. They could also be used to solve technical problems such as foreshortening, and, more generally, to trigger unexpected insights into the two-dimensional representation of the human body.

The production of such nudes became something of an industry in France as the century wore on. Studies of the naked bodies of men, women and children were made available in a variety of poses, as were close-ups of hands and feet. A well-made photograph was expected to show the body under a uniform light which would depict anatomical detail as clearly as possible, though gestures and expressions were also considered to be helpful. Mirrors were commonly used to reveal a body in the round (70).

A more elaborate kind of aid might include props of various kinds, voluminous draperies and fabrics, and possibly some body adornment (71, 81). Sometimes poses loosely approximated or even mimicked those of famous paintings. Auguste Belloc's untitled study of a female nude (69) is uncannily close to Velasquez's *Toilet of Venus*. When it came to these more elaborate treatments of the nude the body was almost inevitably female; mid-nineteenth-century male nudes are extremely rare. In this gender bias, however, photography was simply following the lead of painting, in which the female nude had been the primary focus for five hundred years.

As it was in France that these aids were most widely available, many French artists made use of them. The great romantic painter Eugène Delacroix was a particularly influential enthusiast, not only commissioning photographs and taking some of his own, but writing presciently about the medium. He observed that 'many other artists have had recourse to the daguerreotype to correct errors of vision',[4] and noted that the drawings of certain Renaissance masters such as Marcantonio Raimondi looked wholly unnatural in comparison with photographs. His only complaint was that 'the admirable invention came so late!'[5] He would have marvelled later in the century at the pioneering studies of the body in motion by Muybridge and Marey (107, 118-19, 122), which would win many converts to the idea that the medium revealed new facts.

Another great painter who used photographs as studies for his work was Edgar Degas. A number of his drawings suggest that he had absorbed lessons from Muybridge. Degas himself was an accomplished photographer and his wholly original approach to composition, framing, lighting and subject matter was well in advance of his colleagues, anticipating the casual intimacy of late-twentieth-century photographers (79).

Other Western countries did not offer hospitable climates for the production of such aids, and artists who wished to make use of them had to rely on purchases from France. Strict regulation of the mail made this difficult: 'These beautiful prints are produced with the greatest care, and without any kind of retouching, because of the very special purpose for which they are to be used,' wrote the *Photographic News* in 1880, 'Unfortunately, the majority of artists are obliged to do without them.'[6]

As early as the 1850s in France, there was a certain amount of photographic experimentation with the nude as a subject in its own right. But in England the idea met with little interest and occasional hostility. Those nudes that were produced were very decorous affairs. There was nothing in Roger Fenton's reticent example to ruffle bourgeois feathers (73). Oddly enough, given the moral climate, naked children were particularly popular subjects in both Britain and France (74, 75), and many of the images have a distinct undertow of eroticism.

Kusakabe Kimbei's 1890s staging of a next-to-naked Japanese letter-carrier (83) would have been quite acceptable to European eyes since nakedness was seen as appropriate 'costume' for non-Westerners. The same is true of the anonymous photograph of Iban women posed bare-breasted with various cultural artefacts (77).[7] However F. R. Barton's study of a Motu girl in Papua New Guinea may have been somewhat more unsettling (76). Barton was a colonial administrator among the indigenous Papuans. His ostensibly anthropological subject (in this particular series of images, which was extensive) was tattooing, but his work betrays a sexual obsession with nubile girls. According to anthropologists Maureen MacKenzie and Martha Macintyre, Barton's photographs were not the documentary realism that they seem to be, but 'staged tableaux':

> Moving beyond the scientifically defined boundaries of anthropological study, Barton directed his compositions according to late-nineteenth-century art traditions. The girls become artist's models, choreographed by Barton to emulate the postures of Hellenic sculptures . . .
> . . . The young Papuans become Oriental Odalisques, their sexual attractiveness being cloaked in the Edwardian high-art genre.[8]

The authors point out that tattoos such as the one shown here would not normally have been visible to the gaze of an outsider, which suggests that Barton was exercising his powers exploitively. In photography, we must remind ourselves, photographs of the figure are not always what they seem.

As the century waned, certain photographers began to show an interest in the nude within the context of Symbolist ideas. The figures depicted by the Pictorialists, as they were called, were asexual creatures, ethereal, fleshless (no mere paeans to the flesh', wrote one critic approvingly of Steichen's nudes[9]). Special printing techniques produced hazy and indistinct effects so that the images looked like etchings or lithographs. The models were almost always women, heads turned shyly from the camera (Steichen claims that the women themselves chose to look away). Male nudity was seen for the most part as too blatantly sexual, though boys, who were thought to be less sensually provocative, were acceptable. Adult males were considered suitable for compositions having to do with myth, legend and the ancient world (67).

It is difficult not to accuse the Pictorialists of a surfeit of sentimentality and reactionary thinking, given the radical departures from tradition characteristic of painting of the time, but their earnest efforts did provide a basis for the rebirth of the nude in the early years of the twentieth century. A number of photographers, including Weston and Steichen, went through a phase of moody

Anonymous (French)
Male Nude Study c. 1843
Daguerreotype

and indistinct pictures before embracing the modernist canon. Moreover, the work of some modernists was enriched by Symbolism (72). The French photographer František Drtikol was comfortable with elements of both styles (41, 78).

As we have seen in the introduction, early twentieth-century American nudes tended towards a hard-edged realism. Stieglitz, Weston and Cunningham (84, 93, 92) put moody expressionism behind them and, in Weston's words, strove 'to present objectively the texture, rhythm, form in nature, without subterfuge or evasion in technique or spirit . . .'[10] Delight in geometry and abstraction compensated for the loss of mysticism and emotion. By contrast, a more avant-garde imagination suffused the best European nudes. Man Ray and his colleagues were more interested in breaking free of the realist mode and substituting for it visions from the inner eye – light graphics, montages, solarizations and other

Numa-Blanc
Untitled c. 1856-69
Albumen print

Anonymous
Untitled c. 1890
Albumen print

darkroom manipulations. Even a more conventional figure study was an opportunity to use innovative materials such as cellophane (96).

But these tendencies should not obscure a general climate of support for the subject of the nude, as well as considerable transatlantic cross-fertilization. The best of the Americans exhibited in important exhibitions in Europe and emigrant Europeans brought to North America familiarity with avant-garde art ideas, elegance and a zest for experimentation (89). Newcomers to the U.S. like George Hoyningen-Huene (86), Horst P. Horst (85, 100) and Erwin Blumenfeld (88) worked for prestigious mass-circulation magazines such as *Vogue, Vanity Fair* and *Harper's Bazaar* and their creative influence was widely felt.

British photographers found a somewhat more liberal climate for the nude in the twentieth century. In 1934 Bertram Parks and Yvonne Gregory (95) published *The Beauty of Female Form*, possibly the first book of nudes in Britain which was not connected to the naturist movement.[11] John Havinden made Henry Moore's acquaintance and photographed the sculptor's model **67**

Gwendolyn Ellis in a Mooresque vein (90), while Rosalind Maingot was evidently influenced by Surrealism (87). In terms of an absolutely original vision, however, Bill Brandt was the foremost of the British photographers who took up the subject of the nude (53, 355), situating his models in claustrophobic Victorian rooms which seem at odds with the sensuous nature of the flesh.

U.S. photographer Ruth Bernhard's delicately rendered nudes of the 1960s were made in response to tendencies she saw in Western culture which worked to debase and exploit the bodies of women (98). She hoped to compensate for a tide of photographs which were 'sordid and cheap' by producing images with rhythmic, fluid lines, evocative of music and poetry.[12] Bathed in soft natural light, her bodies are at peace with themselves and with each other.

Richard Crawshay
Turkish Bath
c. 1870
Ambrotype

Auguste Belloc
Untitled c. 1850
Albumen print

A similarly rhythmic orchestration of line and shape animates Dianora
Niccolini's 1970s black male nudes. She, too, hoped to oppose the deeply rooted
belief that the naked body was 'evil, dirty and therefore must be hidden –
especially the male body'.[13] One solution was to heroicize the masculine
physique and draw parallels with works of art (101). Indeed, the texture of the
superb body in Niccolini's image is – thanks to a partial solarization – more akin
to bronze than flesh. The tight cropping, which compresses the body inside the
frame, is highly effective as a means of creating pictorial tension, particularly as
Niccolini stops just at the point where further fragmentation would compromise
a sense of the body's wholeness. By comparison with Niccolini's bronze texture,
Robert Mapplethorpe's splayed male figure is flesh incarnate (94). While her
model suggests a statue, his looks like a crucified figure, rising above the head of
the viewer. Here the photographer indulges in a deliberate iconographic   **69**

A. Vignola
Untitled c. 1900
Albumen print

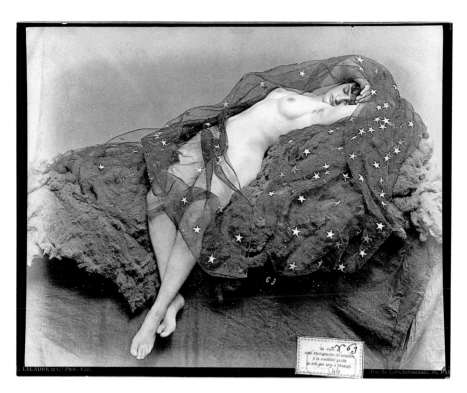

J. E. Lecadre
Untitled c. 1871-96
Albumen print

ambiguity, between the sacred (the form of the cross) and the profane (the eroticized flesh).[14]

Such darker themes characterize much late twentieth-century photography of the naked figure. This is partly in reaction to what are perceived as particularly troubled times for the body, and partly because nudity has become such a commonplace motif in popular culture and so ubiquitous in advertising that serious photographers believe that some shock therapy is needed in order to reclaim the body for art.

Photographers are not alone in their efforts to reinvest the body with humanity; many contemporary painters, video, performance and installation artists, and dancers express similar sentiments. Photographer Philip Trager's image of dancer Marika Blossfeldt portrays a vulnerable, tormented creature, **71**

André Garban
Woman with Skull, Paris c. 1930
Gelatin silver bromide

(right) Roger Fenton
Partially Draped Nude 1850s
Albumen print

like a young bird abandoned by its mother (102). This and other Trager dance images warn that the world is no longer a nurturing, natural habitat.

Spanish photographer Javier Vallhonrat sought out the gifted French dancer Dominique Abel to give shape to his ideas about the human 'possession' of space – the two-dimensional possession by the photographer, the three-dimensional possession by the dancer (105). Vallhonrat believes that the universal use, or

rather abuse, of photography has cheated human beings of the ability to perceive

Louise Biender-Mestro
Untitled c. 1895-1914
Albumen print

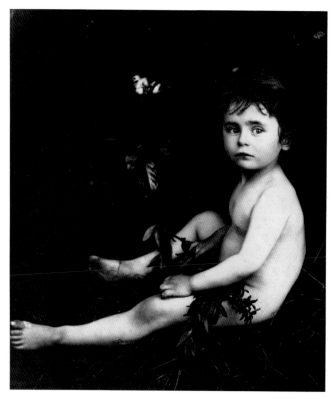

Eveleen Myers
Harold c. 1890
Platinum print

and experience space in depth; increasingly we dwell in a flattened, two-dimensional image-world. With his supple collaborator, Vallhonrat sets out to redress this imbalance, directing her to embody simple geometric shapes – in this instance the triangle – with her volume. Thus can art, thus *must* art 'approach and challenge the pure signs of mathematical rationality.'[15]

Vallhonrat's compatriot Humberto Rivas has chosen a less theatrical mode for his portrayal of a somewhat androgynous young woman (104). He allows her frank gaze to engage us directly. Rivas employs a black background to throw his **75**

Captain F. R. Barton
Motu girl paddling a canoe c. 1890
Modern print from glass plate original

subject's pale form into sharp relief, while the rumpled sheet lends the image a sense of depth and relieves its starkness.

Among the most inventive late twentieth-century nudes are those produced in the 1970s and 1980s by the U. S. photographer Lee Friedlander (97). When they appeared in book form in 1991 critics found them difficult to assess: 'They're not just different from the coy nudes one sees in titillating magazines,' wrote Ingrid Sischy in the book's afterword, 'They're not like the usual nudes one finds in an art context either.'[16] There was the requisite attention to formal concerns of line and volume, cropping and angling, but equally there was a frank

Anonymous
Untitled (Borneo) c. 1890
Albumen print

77

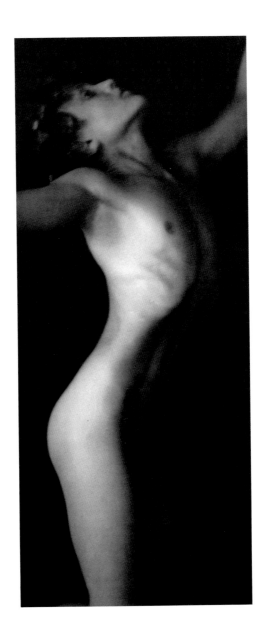

František Drtikol
Male Nude 1921
Gelatin silver print

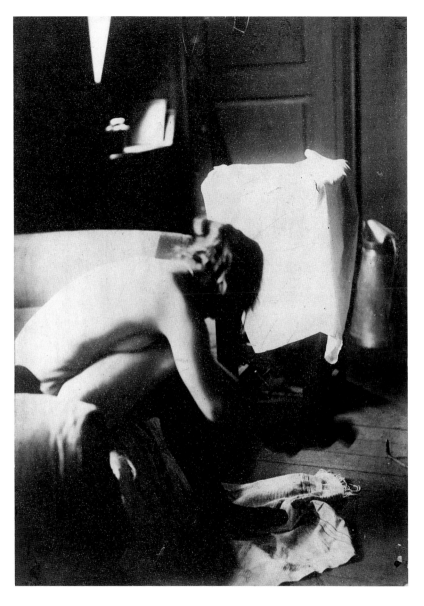

Edgar Degas
Seated Nude 1895
Gelatin silver print

Vincenzo Galdi
Untitled c. 1890
Albumen print

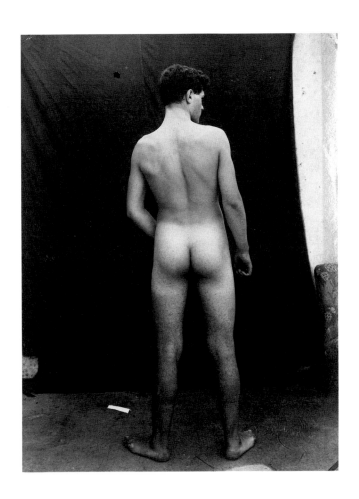

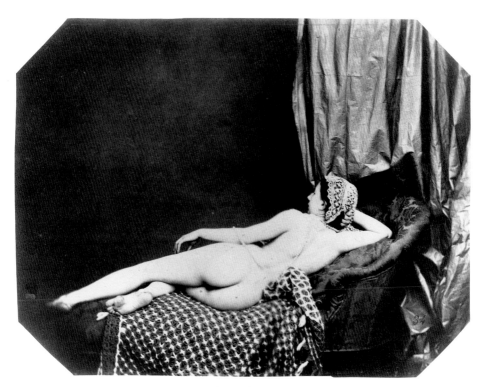

Auguste Belloc
Untitled c. 1854
Albumen print

acceptance of 'flesh and blood' – bruises, scratches, birthmarks, veins visible under the skin, unruly body hair – a side of corporeality which is so often played down. The poses struck by the women are wholly unorthodox – they stretch themselves like cats across the frame and on occasion seem virtually to tie themselves in knots – yet they never appear forced or uncomfortable in front of the camera.

There are echoes here of earlier exponents of the female nude – Eugène Atget, E. J. Bellocq, Weston and Brandt – and one senses that Friedlander was quite consciously paying homage to his inventive predecessors without compromising his own path. His work reminds us that the photographic nude is a subject which can always be revitalized. □

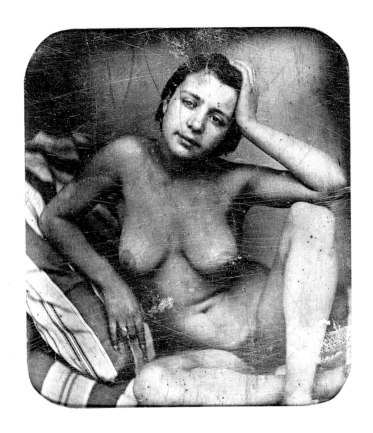

Anonymous (French)
Nude Woman with Cushion c. 1855
Stereo daguerreotype

(right) Kusakabe Kimbei
Man Conveying a Daimeo Letter c. 1890
Albumen print

Alfred Stieglitz
Georgia O'Keeffe, A Portrait 1918
Palladium print

Horst P. Horst
Nude c. 1952
Gelatin silver print

George Hoyningen-Huene
Untitled c. 1930
Gelatin silver print

Rosalind Maingot
Untitled c. 1935
Gelatin silver print

Erwin Blumenfeld
Untitled c. 1952
Solarized gelatin silver print

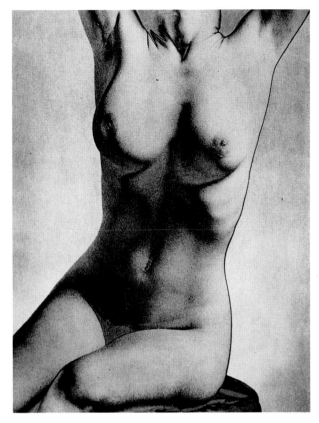

Konrad Cramer
Untitled c. 1938
Solarized gelatin silver print

John Havinden
Untitled (Gwendolyn Ellis) 1930s
Gelatin silver print

Florence Henri
Nude 1938
Gelatin silver print

Imogen Cunningham
Nude 1932
Gelatin silver print

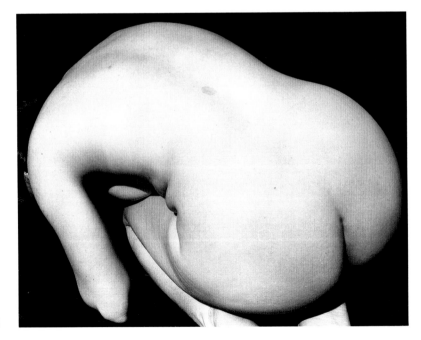

Edward Weston
Charis Nude 1936
Gelatin silver print

Robert Mapplethorpe
Derrick Cross 1983
Gelatin silver print

Yvonne Gregory
Untitled *c.* 1930
Toned silver print

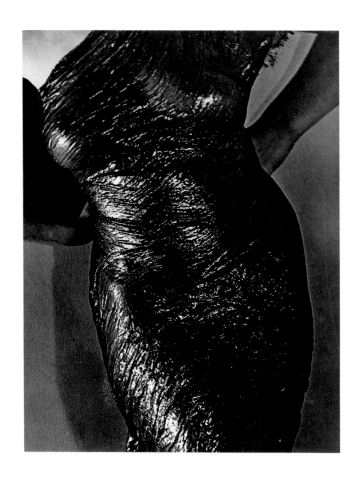

Man Ray
Torso c. 1930
Gelatin silver print

Lee Friedlander
Nude, Phoenix, Arizona 1978
Gelatin silver print

Ruth Bernhard
Two Forms 1963
Gelatin silver print

Robert Mapplethorpe
Philip Prioleau 1984
Gelatin silver print

Horst P. Horst
Male Nude c. 1950
Gelatin silver print

Dianora Niccolini
Untitled 1975
Solarized gelatin silver print

Sally Mann
Shiva 1991
Gelatin silver print

Philip Trager
Tamar Rogoff, Distillations I-V;
Marika Blossfeldt 1992
Gelatin silver print

103

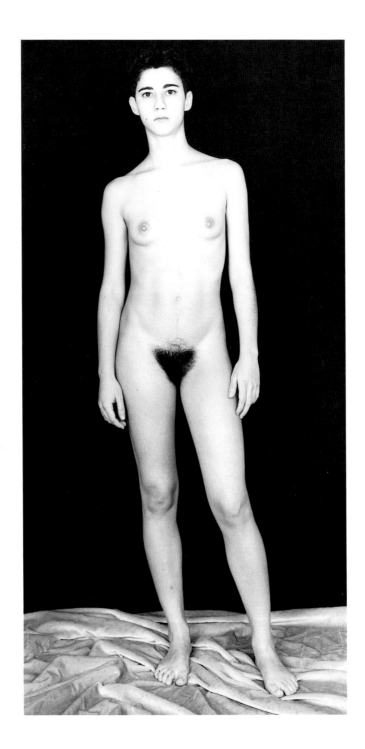

Javier Vallhonrat
Triangle 1987
Gelatin silver print

Humberto Rivas
Eva 1990
Gelatin silver print

105

PROBES

The uses to which photographs may be put are so numerous that we anticipate for it a very foremost place among the scientific appliances of the age.

The Photographic News, 6 January 1865

It is the field of medicine which first comes to mind when we think of probing the mysterious inner workings of the human body. In the mid-nineteenth century, medical journals were full of enthusiasm for photography, and doctors responded to the call by initiating photographic experiments in almost every area of medicine – anatomy, physiology, histology, pathology and the more ambiguous field of mental illness.

Not all physicians were enthusiasts, however. For those who had long depended on the primacy of touch in the diagnosis of illness, photography was of limited interest. Even those who were appreciative of its powers saw it as a secondary or back-up technique, a way of validating what had already been seen: 'The value of the art of photography to medicine and science [is] . . . as a means of recording the experience of the eye,' noted the *Medical Times and Gazette* in 1866, though one area in which photography was uncontested was photomicrography.[1]

As in certain other branches of science, such as botany and zoology, medical photography had to compete with a well-established tradition of illustration dating back to the Renaissance. Some exponents of drawing resisted photography on principle, arguing that the hand would always remain superior to the lens. Others foresaw a time when photography would catch up and surpass drawing. Its superior strengths were outlined in the *Photographic News*: 'First, its cheapness; second, its simplicity; third, its power of infinite reproduction,

Etienne-Jules Marey
Man Walking 1890-91
Chronophotography on moving film

and fourth, last, and most important of all, its absolute truth and fidelity. It *cannot* lie.'[2]

One of the advantages of medical drawings over photography was that they observed well-established conventions whereby one body part was made distinct from another. In drawings of dissected bodies, for example, clear lines and different shadings made boundaries obvious, whereas photographs were difficult to read for those without experience on cadavers. In addition, many textbook illustrations were schematic or diagrammatic, and here photography could not possibly compete.

Yet even the superbly honed skills of nineteenth-century illustrators only partly explain the primacy of the drawing: a further and important factor was that highly elaborate techniques of reproduction were in place to disseminate these illustrations. Fine lithographs were plentiful and cheap in the 1820s and 1830s. And though engravings and etchings were more expensive, they were still available if needed; for the depiction of certain skin conditions, for example, stipple engraving and aquatint were considered ideal. The mid-nineteenth-century scientific photograph, on the other hand, was not a crystal-clear document. Only late in the century would reasonable tonal reproduction become a practical option. Before then, doctors and students relied on textbooks filled with drawings. Where we do find very early medical photographs, as in the work of L. Haase of Berlin in the 1860s, they serve as a kind of record-keeping of orthopaedic patients' conditions, rather than as a body of imagery which would be communicated to a wider circle (255).

Nonetheless, the potential of photography was recognized. The journals continually reported novel applications or suggested paths which might be explored. In the 1840s a British physician and amateur photographer, Hugh Welch Diamond, began to make portraits of the insane, in whose faces (in keeping with the widespread faith in physiognomy) he hoped to register 'the permanent cloud, or the passing storm, or the sunshine of the soul'.[3] Working in the same area some twenty years later, with a more sophisticated notion of what photography could achieve, Dr Noyes of New York experimented with composite portraits of mentally ill patients (each composite being made up of a number of patients' faces), in the expectation that his tool would reveal what

108 patients suffering a similar affliction had in common.

Facial expression was also the subject of unusual work undertaken in the mid-1850s by the French neurologist Guillaume-Benjamin Duchenne (17). Aided by the photographer Adrien Tournachon (brother of Nadar), Duchenne de Boulogne, as he is known, analysed facial expressions by applying an electrical current to specific muscles (116). Also a subscriber to physiognomy, Duchenne set out to construct a vocabulary of facial expressions, each of which corresponded to a specific emotion, or, as he put it, 'an experimental living picture of the passions'.[4] The principles whereby human beings expressed their emotions were 'universal and immutable' and created by God. Duchenne saw his findings as invaluable to artists; without understanding the mechanism of physiognomy, he argued, no one could expect to render expressions accurately.[5]

In 1879 the *Photographic News* described a 'pulsograph', by which 'the state of the heart' could be measured, while in Frankfurt a Dr Stein overcame what he saw as the defect of the Marey sphygmograph, which was that of friction caused by the movement of the pen against the paper as the pulse was traced; in place of the pen the doctor substituted 'rays of light' and for the ordinary piece of paper, a sheet photo-sensitively treated.[6] A few years later we read of St Bartholomew's Hospital in London purchasing 'a photographic apparatus' to instruct students.[7]

In 1888 Professor Cohn of Breslau produced 'marvellously detailed photographs of diseased eyes'. Cohn used 'the magnesium flash light, and, remarkably enough, the patients are none the worse'.[8] Sadly, Cohn's work, and that of other pioneers of whom we have written reports, seems to have vanished without trace.[9]

As stated earlier, the first photographs of sick patients were taken in the manner of portraits, as if the dignity of the sitter and his or her identity as a person were the primary consideration. Gradually, however, photographers dispensed with the props and decorative treatments and focused closely on the diseased section or abnormality, on a cancerous growth, skin condition, wound, deformity and so on (254, 257).

A physician of 1894 interested in the role of photography would be amazed by the panorama of imaging systems and techniques available a century later. Certainly any reservations he might have had concerning the relative merits of drawing over photography would have been long dispelled.[10]

In *The Fabric of the Body* (1992), a study of European traditions of anatomical illustration, authors K. B. Roberts and J. D. W. Tomlinson explain that photographs are now considered indispensable in the instruction of anatomy. They give as prime examples Ralph T. Hutchings's 1977 studies of the muscles of the back of the hand (121). Having been given both the photographs and an actual dissected specimen, the student 'should have no difficulty in identifying the muscles of this region.'[11]

The elaborate dissections required by modern anatomy and the technical problems they pose for photography call for exceedingly ingenious and time-consuming solutions. Hutchings took seven years to photograph all the surgical procedures for a book dealing with the reconstructive surgery of the rheumatoid hand. For a photograph of a skeleton, he flashed his light source 250 times over a 180-degree semicircular path to make one single exposure. Such care allowed him to 'wrap his light around each bone'.[12] In fact, this painstaking technique dates back, naturally in a more primitive form, to the 1880s, when it was called 'painting with light'. It was a solution to the problem of very slow film.

The all-embracing eye of the camera, as Hutchings put it, has taken many forms in the new medicine. A modern physician or researcher has recourse to a battery of techniques with which to read the inner body. A scintigram, or gamma camera scan, involves a radioactive tracer in order to map the brain and spinal cord (130). A false-colour scanning electron micrograph (SEM) may be employed to show a section through the inner ear, the cells of the lens of the eye (133), or bony lamellae on the femur (131). A transmission electron micrograph (TEM) will show the human serum protein molecule (134). A polarized light micrograph may be used to show the structure of bone.

For the layman, the technical terms themselves defy understanding: false-colour, freeze-fracture transmission electron micrography; digital subtraction angiography; venography, or, if one prefers, phlebography; Schlieren photography (showing the air turbulence caused by sneezing, coughing or simply exhaling [136]); and Colourvir X-rays. So rapid are advances in technology that certain of the techniques put at the disposal of physicians have yet to find specific uses.

Following the pioneering and justly acclaimed endoscopic photography
produced by Lennart Nilsson in the 1960s, the technique has become familiar.[13]

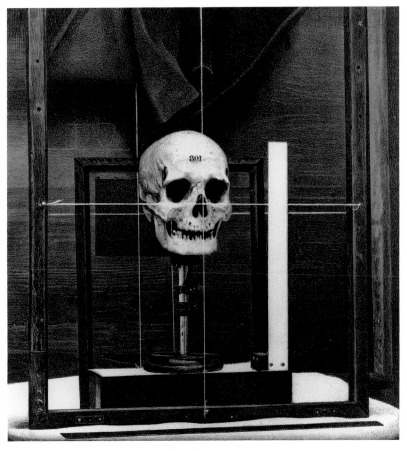

Julius Rien & Co.
Arrangement for taking composite photographs of skulls 1885
Albumen print

Here, Alexander Tsiaras provides an endoscopic image of the human foetus *in vivo* after eleven weeks (*preliminary pages*); it makes clear the extent of the foot's development, which is shown to have been more rapid than that of the leg. The endoscope is a series of lenses with a fibre optic light source which has been inserted through the cervix and manipulated until a 'window' into the amniotic sac is found (that is, an area where the wall is thinner).

Mention must also be made of non-photographic imaging systems which are revolutionizing medicine, notably computed tomography,[14] magnetic resonance[15] and ultrasound,[16] each of which offers specific diagnostic advantages. In some 111 areas the use of conventional photography will disappear. For instance, digital subtraction angiography, used to examine blood vessels, is now supplanting conventional film angiography. But all the new methods are close cousins to photography in that they extend the great medical tradition of naturalistic representation. The alliance of old and new is nowhere better demonstrated than in the digital cadavers of the U.S. National Institutes of Health. These teaching aids, which do away with the need for actual cadavers, are composed of thousands of individual slices (cross-sections from head to foot), each of which is made from an original photograph, thus allowing the student sitting before a computer screen to 'travel' through the length of the body.

As we have seen in the introduction, measurement and classification of the body were central to the emerging discipline of anthropology in the nineteenth century within the context of race and evolution. At that time, the word 'race' encompassed more than different physical characteristics. It connoted moral character, intellectual capacity, even the capacity for 'civilized' behaviour. Because races could be arranged in a hierarchy of superiority, it was thought that photographic documents would help slot each racial group into the grand scheme. One such project called for a study of the 'Typical Races of the British Empire'.[17] An even more ambitious undertaking for an 'Ethnological Photographic Gallery of the Various Races of Man' was begun in the 1870s by photographers working for the *Berliner Gesellschaft für Anthropologie*. This map of man started at the top with the 'Germanic and Teutonic' types and worked downwards, arriving eventually at the Australian aborigines. There was an unconscious racism at work here, and one arbitrary assumption was piled upon another. Notes anthropologist Roslyn Poignant: 'This gradation [of types] is paralleled visually by a transition from dressed to undressed; a line of descent from manufactured clothing via traditional or ceremonial costumes to natural garb of fibre and skin'.[18] Photographs, whose objectivity was accepted at face value, 'proved' to Europeans their own superiority.

The anthropologists T. H. Huxley and John Lamprey were concerned that the typical early ethnological photographs were not, as Huxley put it, 'uniform and well-considered', and that they failed to give 'that precise information respecting the proportions and the conformation of the body' that the ambitious typologies required.[19] The different methods each proposed whereby certain parameters of human bodies could be precisely measured, compared and classified have already been discussed (126, 127). But it should be noted that not all anthropologists subscribed to the anthropometric method. Everard im Thurn, who worked closely with the Indian peoples of Guiana in the 1880s and 1890s, argued that 'the purely physiological photographs of the anthropometrists are merely pictures of lifeless bodies', as misleading a vision of native peoples as 'ordinary photographs of uncharacteristically miserable natives . . . [which] seem comparable to the photographs which one occasionally sees of badly stuffed and distorted animals.'[20]

The human body features as prime subject in the investigations of movement by Eadweard Muybridge and Etienne-Jules Marey, who proved to scientists and artists alike that the evidence of the senses could not be trusted to unravel the secrets of bodies in motion (118-119, 122). Muybridge's method of arresting consecutive phases of motion required a marvellous piece of Victorian electromechanical ingenuity. The *Philadelphia Times* described it in some detail in 1885:

> The photographs are taken by three batteries of cameras, with twelve lenses to each battery. These batteries are placed at right angles to each other [sic] . . . and are all focused on one subject. When the model or object under consideration is photographed, thirty-six negatives are obtained . . . [representing] different stages of muscular action from the three different points of view . . . In this way every inch of a man's or beast's progress can be photographed, no matter what the speed.[21]

Artists were much influenced by what Muybridge's cameras revealed, and debate raged over the implications. Many artists, like Thomas Eakins (119), were willing to revise their conceptions of how bodies in motion should be represented. But not all: 'Mr Muybridge's photographs are, perhaps, rather of indirect importance to the artist, as showing him what actually takes place, than as a direct means of assisting him to represent what the eye actually sees,' wrote the *Photographic News* in 1889.[22] At least one significant voice was raised in agreement: Auguste Rodin rejected the camera's awkward evidence in favour of the artist's right to interpret, citing the more convincing walk of his own *St John the Baptist*.

H. Goulton May
Cerveau Mongolique (*Mongoloid Brain*) c. 1880
Albumen print

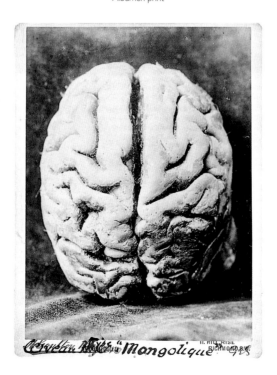

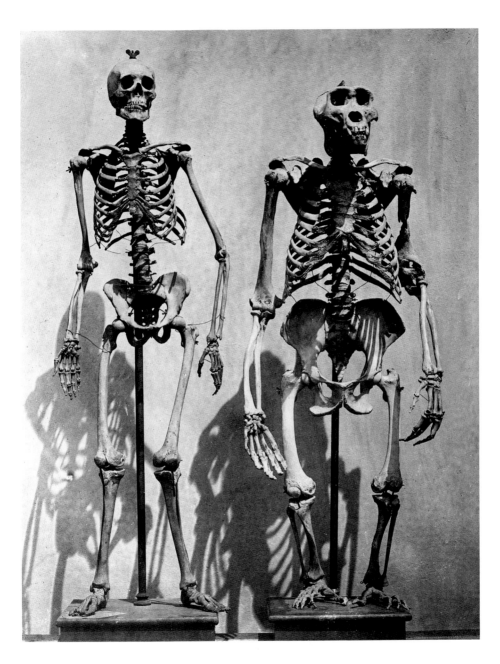

Roger Fenton
Skeleton of Man and the Male Gorilla c. 1861
Albumen print

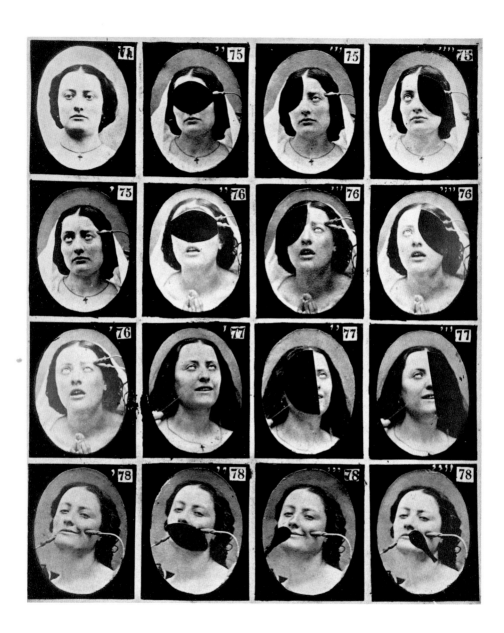

Dr Guillaume-Benjamin Duchenne with Adrien Tournachon
From *Mécanisme de la physionomie humaine ou analyse électro-physiologique de l'expression des passions*
(published 1862) 1852-56
Albumen prints

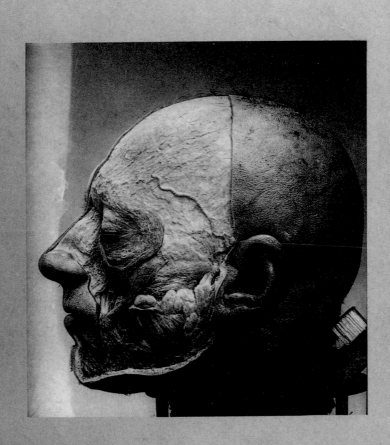

Gesichtsmuskeln durch Formalin-Alcohol-Injection fixirt.

Vorlesung über Kunst-Anatomie W.S. 1904/5.

präp. Topuse.

23

Anonymous
Face Muscles Fixed by a Formalin-alcohol Injection. Lecture on the Art of Anatomy 1904-05
Gelatin silver print

Marey, in turn, would have disagreed with Rodin. His passion for getting at the heart of the movement was equal to Muybridge's and his influence was as great if not greater. We see echoes of his famous 'stick figures' (the result of his subject's wearing a black suit with reflective metal strips or buttons attached to it which alone would be seen in the exposure) metamorphosed in the work of early twentieth-century avant-garde artists – Giacomo Balla, the Bragaglias and Marcel Duchamp, for example. □

(below)
Etienne-Jules Marey
Saut (Jump) 1883
Geometric chronophotograph

(right)
Thomas Eakins
Man jumping, with photographer's notations 1884-85
Albumen print

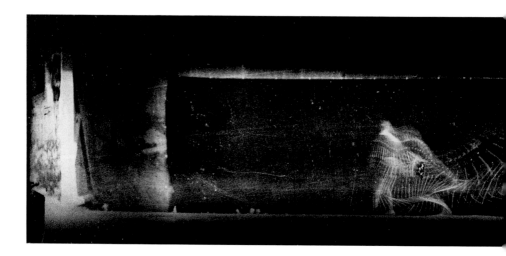

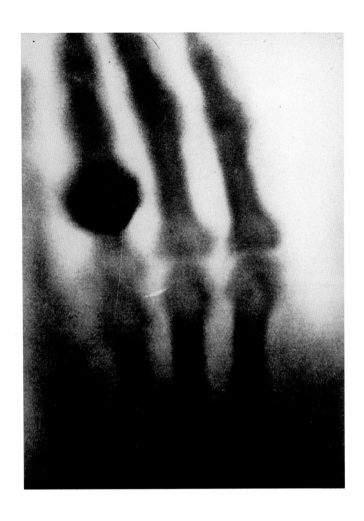

Wilhelm Konrad Röntgen
X-ray of a hand 1895
Transparency

Ralph T. Hutchings
Deep muscles, back of the hand, of a 120-year-old specimen;
two views taken to demonstrate anomalies 1977
Colour transparencies

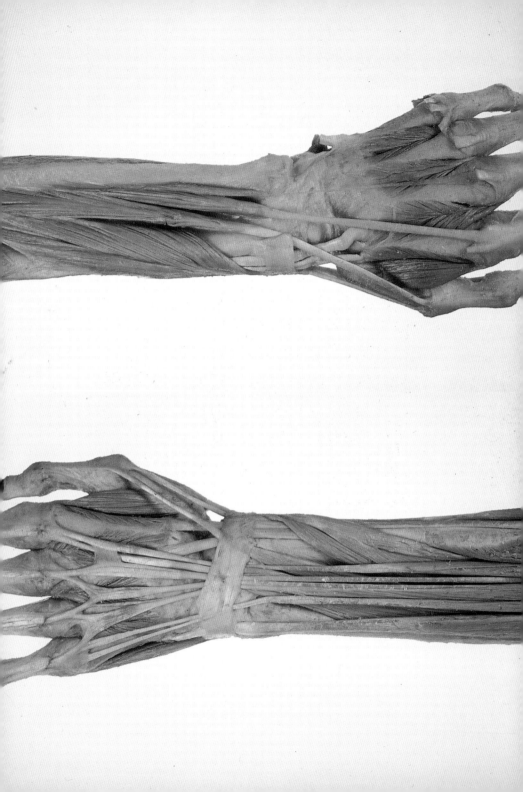

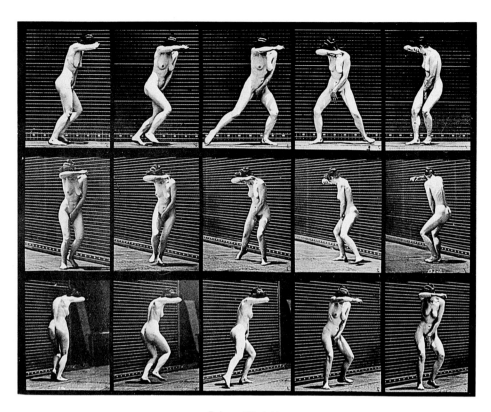

Eadweard Muybridge
Turning around in Surprise and Running Away. Plate 73 from *Animal Locomotion* 1887

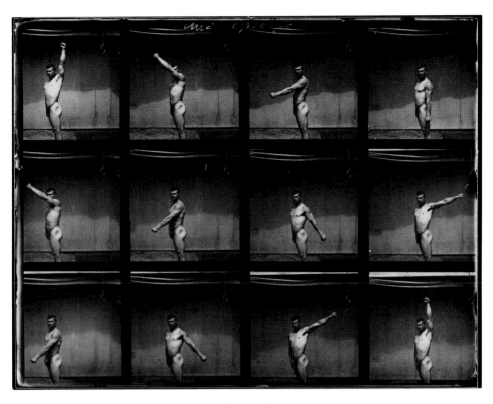

Albert Londe
Mouvement de moulinet du membre supérieur, vitesse modérée (Circular Movement of the Upper Limb, Moderate Speed) c. 1890
Gelatine silver bromide print from glass negative

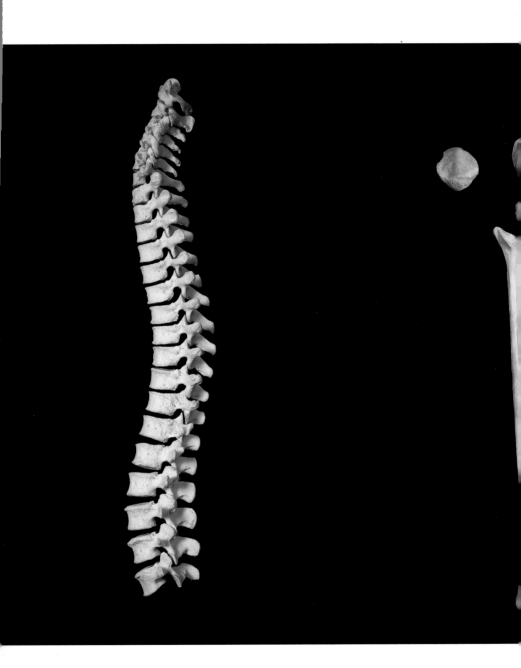

Ralph T. Hutchings
Left to right: Spinal vertebrae (seen from left side). Bones of the lower leg, from behind:
distal end of the femur; tibia; fibula; patella. Ribs 1985
Colour transparencies

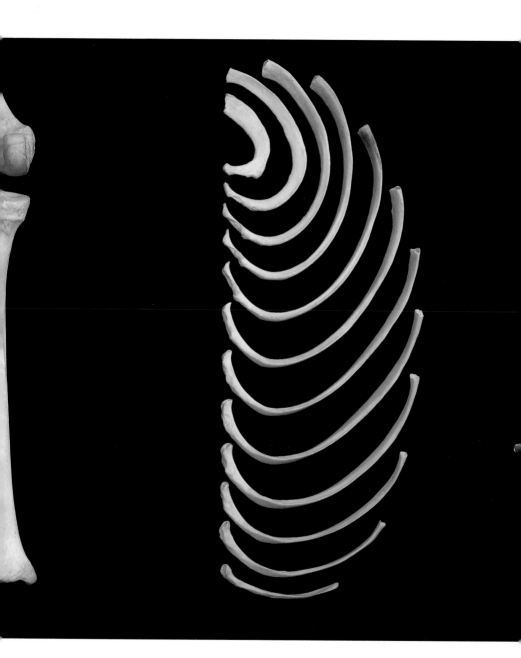

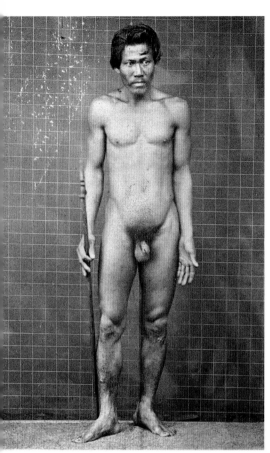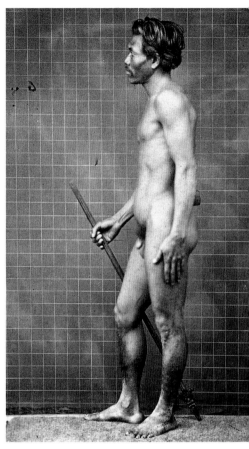

John Lamprey
Malayan male. Anthropometric study *c.* 1868-69
Albumen print

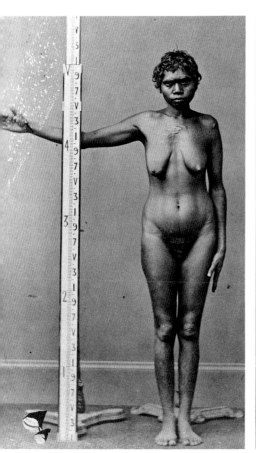 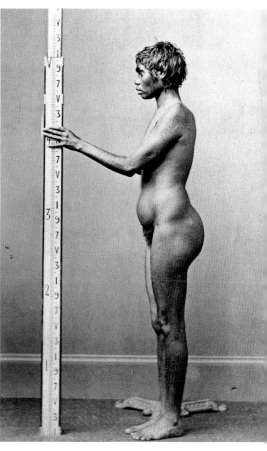

Anonymous
Two of four views of a South Australian aboriginal female, 'Ellen', aged 22.
Photographed according to T. H. Huxley's 'photometric' instructions c. 1870
Albumen prints

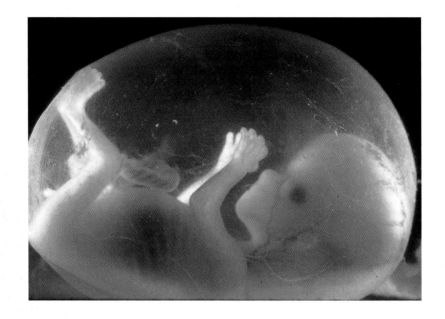

Anonymous
The human foetus after 14 weeks 1984
Colour transparency

Neil Bromhall
The head and hands of a human foetus after 19 weeks 1988
Endoscopic image. Colour transparency

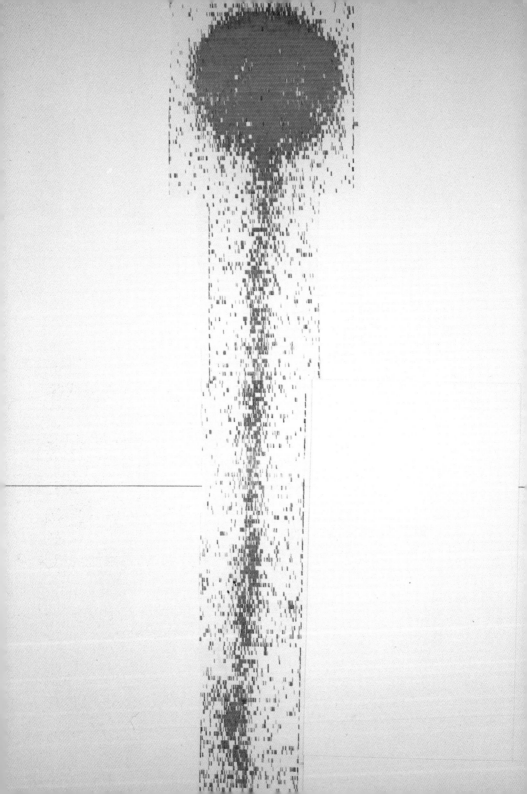

(opposite) Anonymous
Scintigram of the human central nervous system 1987
Gamma camera scan. Colour transparency

Professor Pietro Motta
Compact bone lamellae in the thigh bone 1992
False-colour scanning electron micrograph. Colour transparency

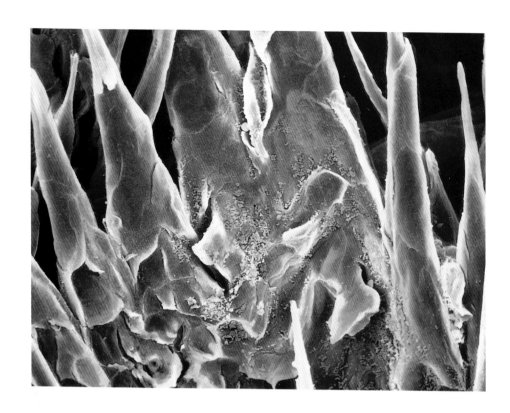

Professor Pietro Motta
Filiform papillae on the surface of the tongue 1992
False-colour scanning electron micrograph. Colour transparency

Professor Pietro Motta
Cells of the lens of the eye 1992
False-colour scanning electron micrograph. Colour transparency

Professor Werner Villiger
Transmission electron micrograph of the human serum protein molecule 1986
Colour transparency

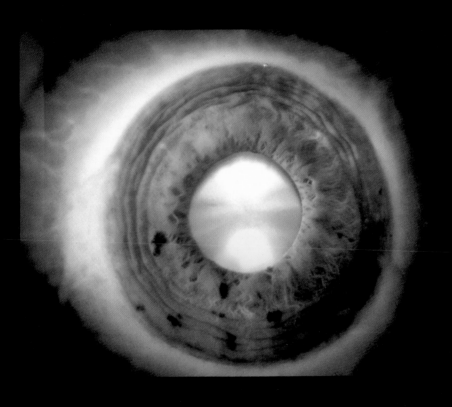

Ralph Eagle
Macrophotograph showing light brown iris (human autopsy specimen) 1985
Colour transparency

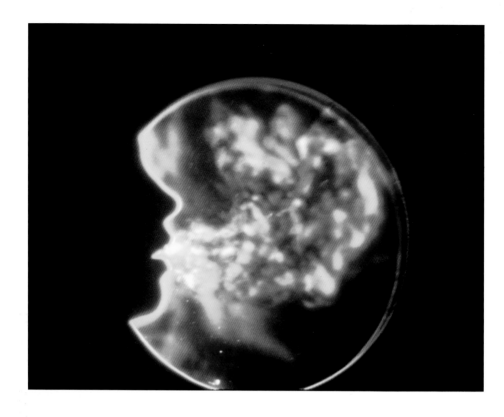

Dr Gary Settles
Schlieren photograph of a person exhaling, showing the air turbulence that such an action causes 1985
Colour transparency

Harold Edgerton
Multiple-flash photo of golfer Bobby Jones c. 1935
Gelatin silver print

FLESH

The twentieth century has restored and deepened the notion of flesh,
that is, of animate body.

MAURICE MERLEAU-PONTY
'Man and Adversity', 1964

'Flesh' has been to the twentieth century what
the rarefied 'figure' was to the nineteenth. For
nineteenth-century photographers of the nude,
mind was the great and worthy faculty, body merely
the lowly vehicle which housed and transported it. Their
wish was to ennoble the human being by rising above
brute corporeal fact. Flesh, which represented all that was
base in man, was explored only by the medical photographer
when, in sickness, it gave proof of its own corruptibility.

It is flesh in the figurative or metaphoric sense that is implied in our usage
here: 'flesh and blood', the whole physical substance of the body – muscle,
organ, fluid, bone. The French poet Paul Valéry once said, 'The deepest thing
in man is the skin,'[1] and the images which follow show the wisdom of
this observation.

Naturally enough, the fragment is often the preferred approach for
photographers concerned with the flesh; the subject seems to call for extreme
close-ups of scars, birthmarks, lumps, bumps, creases and hairs, such as we see
in the imagery of Robert Davies (140, 141). It was the unexpected textures and
shapes which resulted from large-scale blow-ups of fruit and vegetable surfaces
that prompted Davies to focus on human skin, in particular tiny areas which
have generally received little attention. Isolated from the rest of the body these
cavities and protuberances take on a strange aspect, suggesting alien landscapes
rather than familiar human forms.

>>>

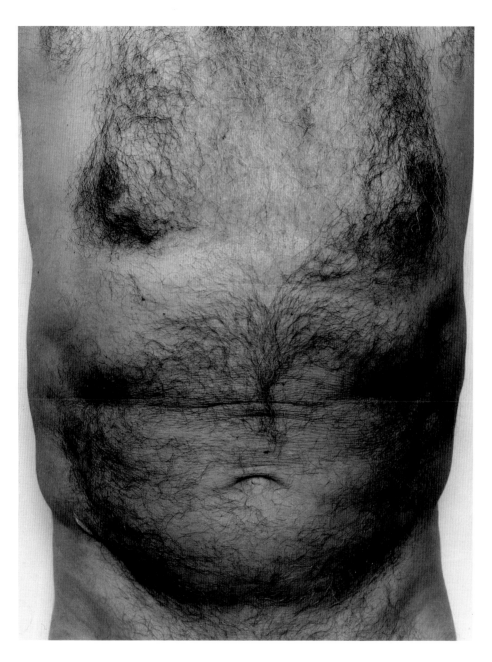

John Coplans
Self-portrait 1984
Gelatin silver print

139

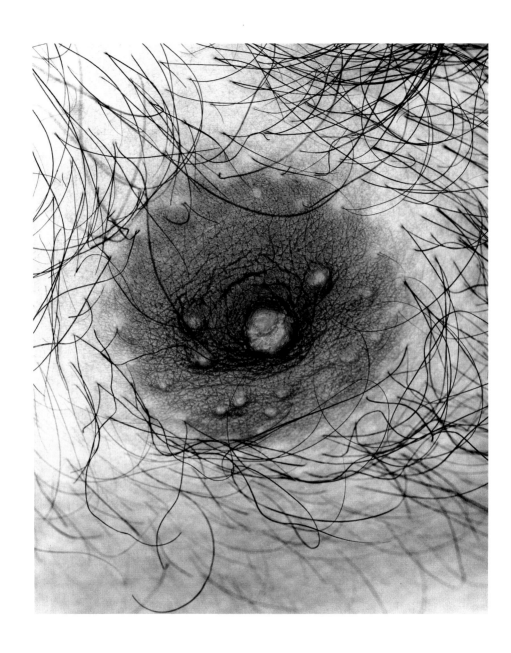

Robert Davies
Nipple I 1992
Gelatin silver print

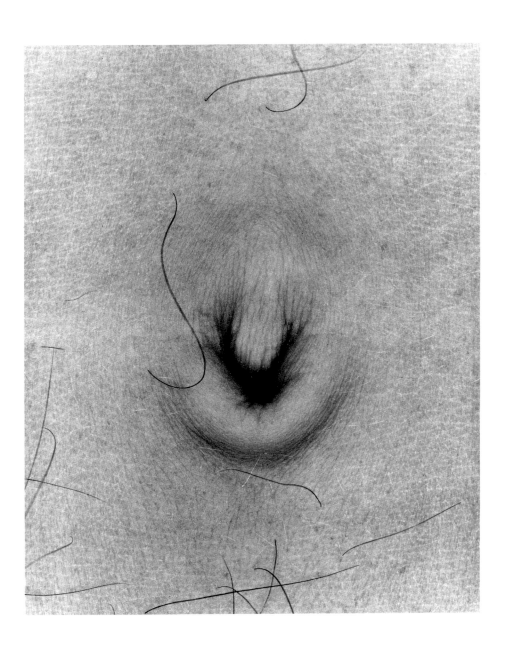

Robert Davies
Belly Button 1 1992
Gelatin silver print

With John Coplans's fragmented self-portraits, the viewer is on more familiar ground; there is no question of anything but notions of 'body' springing to mind when we are confronted with this massive trunk of male flesh (139). I say 'trunk' rather than 'torso' because of the sense it suggests of what is densely packed inside – hard-working organs, reliable systems of plumbing and communications. Understandably the trunk is somewhat the worse for wear, having faithfully transported its master's contents for almost three-quarters of a century.

But this is a body which can also laugh at itself – nipples which are eyes, a navel which mimics a petulant mouth. This picture's forthright acceptance of the physical facts is of a completely different order from the idealized versions of the body which vie for attention from a thousand billboards and magazines. Coplans's torso, densely matted with hair, dotted with moles and marks, scarred and lined with age, yet still defiantly vertical, stands as an indictment of this other, flesh-denying practice, which leads people to fear and belittle their own unique physicality.

Flesh is also dealt with boldly and honestly in the colossal Polaroid composites of Chuck Close, some of which are seventeen feet wide and some seven feet high (151). There is nothing coy or flirtatious in the gaze of the model in a Close nude; poses and expressions are frank and open, inviting clinical examination. As each of the panels which make up the composites (up to five in a horizontal format) is made from a single Polaroid negative of the same size, there is virtually none of the grain characteristic of huge blow-ups, and detail borders on the microscopic. Unexpectedly, perhaps, the gargantuan scale of the bodies strips them of erotic overtones, and we are left to scrutinize the flesh with a more objective eye.

Close's strategy calls to mind 'The Physical Self', an exhibition curated by the filmmaker Peter Greenaway in 1992 at the Boymans-van Beuningen Museum, Rotterdam. Among the original artworks (paintings, drawings and photographs – including the above-mentioned Coplans image) and functional implements, Greenaway interspersed displays (in glass cases!) of living, naked men and women. These functioned as 'templates', reminders of the fundamental 'givens' of the human body, against which the artworks – that is, the cultural representations and interpretations – could be compared and considered.

Raoul Hausmann, the famous 'Dadasoph' of Berlin, artist, writer and poet, would have approved of contemporary efforts to come to grips with the body; by 1927 Hausmann had decided to devote himself to photography, convinced that its lucid eye, unencumbered by the stale visions of Art, could offer humanity a fresh consciousness of itself (144, 145).

Flesh is seen differently, perhaps more existentially, in two images from the late 1920s and early 1930s. In the first, an image of a woman's body by Germaine Krull (146), flesh is seen as a constricting garment; the model wears her 'suit' uncomfortably, as if chafed by it. By comparison, the naked male in the image by Rudemine (147) seems to revel in his elastic suit of flesh.

That flesh is a burden which inevitably accompanies age is the message conveyed by Emmet Gowin's frank study of his wife Edith (157). It comes as a shock to realize how rarely in photography we are allowed to share in such intimacy. Here is a body seen by a lover and husband of long standing, a vulnerable body, weary and resigned, and without a shred of vanity or self-consciousness. Edith's wholehearted trust in her spouse is evident; she virtually embraces the camera. 'I could be myself just as I was at that moment,' she wrote recently, 'and yet, I could be something which only existed in the photograph.'[2] There is a certain beauty here too, not the stock, formulaic beauty of the glossy magazine, but a radiance nonetheless.

Gowin had been photographing Edith since 1961, possibly inspired by the example of his teacher Harry Callahan, who had himself begun an extended portrait of his own wife, Eleanor, in the 1940s. Here, in an image which hints at the unfathomable wonder of childbirth, she is seen pregnant with their daughter Barbara (148).

It is common for parents to train their cameras on the bodies of their offspring; it is far less usual for children to do the same thing to their parents. A mother's aged body is brought into close focus through the lens of the French photographer Yves Trémorin (164, 165). Hélène Trémorin's massive thighs here take on the character of something deeply rooted, venerable and ancient, like a gnarled oak, while her pendulous breasts seem to flow earthward with the consistency of lava. We are culturally conditioned to see aged flesh as decrepit and wasting, but Trémorin's respectful vision invests it instead with grandeur and solidity.

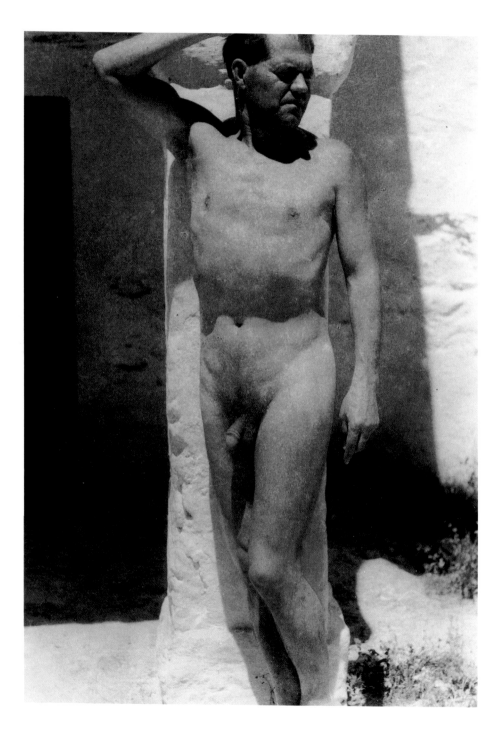

Raoul Hausmann
Allemagne 1931
Gelatin silver print

Raoul Hausmann
Self-portrait 1931
Gelatin silver print

145

Germaine Krull
Nude c. 1928-29
Gelatin silver print

Rudemine
Male nude c. 1930
Gelatin silver print

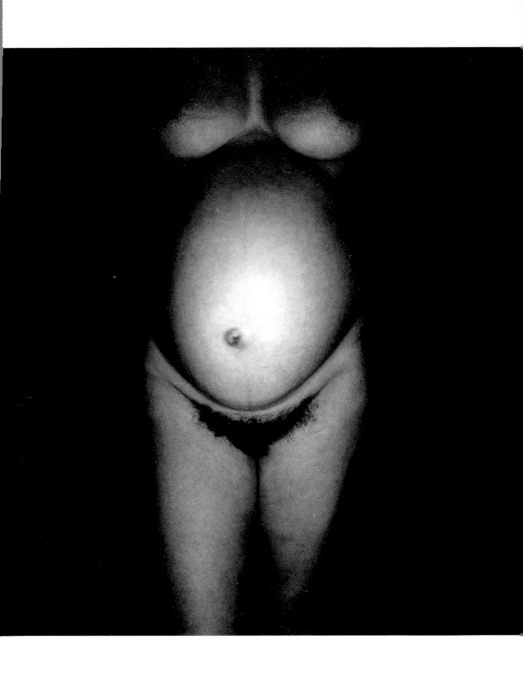

Harry Callahan
Eleanor, Chicago 1949
Gelatin silver print

Imogen Cunningham
Pregnant Nude 1959
Gelatin silver print

Regina DeLuise
Nude on Tire Swing, Northport, NY 1991
Platinum/palladium print

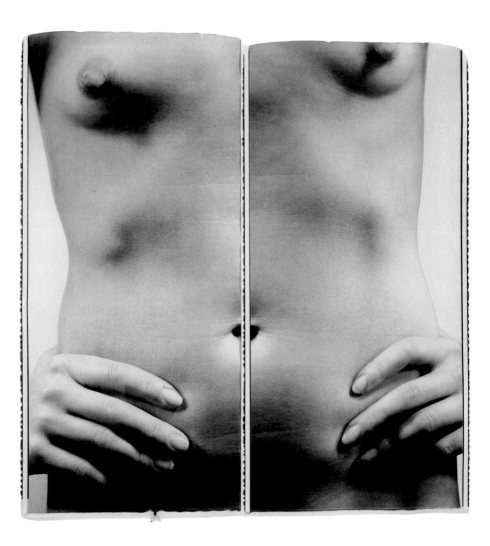

Regina DeLuise
Stephanie in Chair, NYC 1981
Platinum/palladium print

Jed Devine
Emmy Showering, Maine 1980
Palladium print

Regina DeLuise's photographs of women are equally serene reflections on the nature of the flesh, although her models are mere saplings by comparison with Tremorin's venerable subject. In the first of two images (150) a semi-nude young woman swings on a tyre, the taut hard fibre of the rope in counterpoint to the soft rounded contours of her body. There is a delicate balance here between the play of abstract form and attention to the textural nuances of the flesh. In the second (*left*), a young woman sits unselfconsciously for an intimate portrait, gazing into the middle distance. How different this is from the standard male voluptuary approach to the female body, in which the primary focus is inevitably on accentuated curves of breasts and buttocks. We are reminded that sensuality can move us quite independently of eroticism.

Sally Mann
Punctus 1992
Gelatin silver print

The bodies of childhood and adolescence, with all their tribulations, are the primary, sustained focus of contemporary U. S. photographers Jock Sturges and Sally Mann, each of whom has produced an oeuvre of psychological intensity and formal elegance. Fundamental to both visions of youthful flesh is a thorough familiarity with their subjects: Sturges has been photographing the same nudist families in France year after year, watching the children grow into young adults (158-60). Mann photographs her own children negotiating the turbulent waters of childhood (*left* and *below*). Both photographers have settled on a holistic approach, believing that too close a focus on the physical body risks leaving the person behind. Their work should remind us that the purely physical dimension of flesh is only one thread in the body's fabric. □

Sally Mann
Last Light 1990
Gelatin silver print

John Coplans
Self-portrait 1984
Gelatin silver print

Emmet Gowin
Edith, Danville, Virginia 1973
Toned silver print

Jock Sturges
Arianne and François; Montalivet, France 1992
Gelatin silver print

Jock Sturges
Gaële, Marine, Valentin and Marie-Claude; Montalivet, France 1987
Gelatin silver print

Jock Sturges
Danielle; Montalivet, France 1989
Toned silver print

Richard Sadler
John at Arles 1981
Gelatin silver print

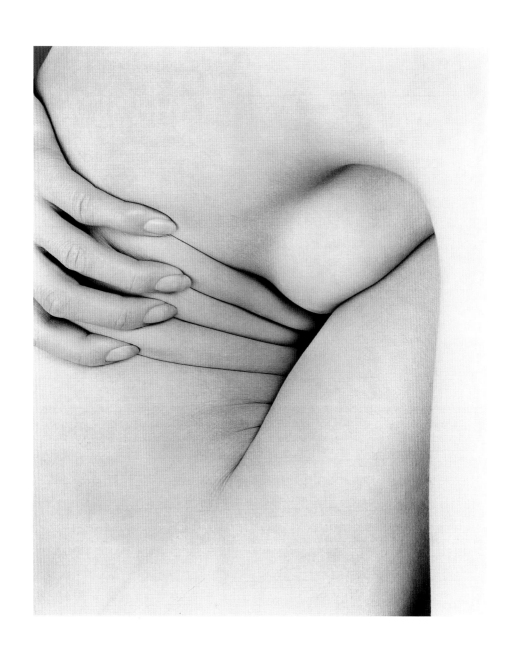

Pierre Radisic
Marilou 1984
Gelatin silver print

Ernestine Ruben
Wrinkles in Back 1984
Gelatin silver print

Yves Trémorin
De cette femme 1985-86
Selenium-toned silver print

Yves Trémorin
De cette femme 1985-86
Selenium-toned silver print

PROWESS

It is strange that no one has thought of taking an instantaneous camera to the recent fight. Such is the interest in the event, the photos would have sold like wildfire.

The Photographic News, 13 January 1888

In the nineteenth century, prowess was defined as an essentially masculine attribute. It connoted certain qualities of 'manly vigour': boldness, bravery, strength and fortitude. In twentieth-century usage, this gender specificity has been substantially eroded; now the term is more likely to signify physical ability rather than virility, dexterity rather than brute strength, expertise rather than fearlessness. A century ago a female bodybuilder with rippling muscles would have been considered a travesty of nature, a sideshow freak. Now an image of a highly developed female physique, such as the photograph of Lisa Lyon by Robert Mapplethorpe (200), scarcely raises an eyebrow.

Prowess in the nineteenth century was also class based: 'gentlemen' had prowess. In Paris, at mid-century, the entrepreneur Triat opened private gymnasiums in which rows of disciplined gymnasts, their muscled torsos stripped to the waist, performed quasi-balletic movements before spectators of the opposite sex. 'La culture physique' was a group or collective activity rather than the individual regimen that it has become today.

To modern eyes, the earliest photographs of sporting activities look somewhat ridiculous. The need for lengthy exposures meant that pictures had to be made in studios, for the most part with backgrounds which were often wholly inappropriate to the sport depicted, so that a skater could be seen whizzing

Anonymous
Sturgess, the Champion Walker c. 1890
Cigarette card

along the ice in front of a lush summery landscape. Nothing could really be *in* motion, and while a contortionist (176) or two wrestlers (175) posed no problems, a moving body or thing, such as a ball, had to be held up with wire or thread and later retouched out in the negative, with for the most part wholly unconvincing results.

Generally, the spectacle of sport as we know it – of teams of highly conditioned bodies locked in combat – did not yet exist in the public sphere. Moreover, ordinary Europeans and Americans did not yet have access to exhibitions and museums where they could study the bodies of Greek and Roman statuary or those of Renaissance painting and sculpture. The era of the photographically illustrated newspaper and review was also in the future. In short, the familiarity of the average citizen with the superbly conditioned athletic body was minimal. Superstrong men were visible to the masses at funfairs and carnivals, but they were regarded as freaks rather than as normal men with well-developed physiques. **167**

The cult of the sports celebrity really begins in the mid-1860s with the mass-produced *cartes de visite* (276), calling-card-sized photographs of famous athletes which were inexpensive to buy and fun to exchange, not unlike baseball cards today. Photographs of gymnasts and circus performers were particularly popular. People relished the fact that they were seeing real people, rather than the idealized representations familiar from prints, because it suggested that the well-developed body was within their own reach.

One of the late-nineteenth-century forces which would influence people's attitudes towards their bodies was naturism, a European movement which sought to counter the ill-effects on the human body of the industrial revolution. Large numbers of people were encouraged to take up exercise in the open air, by hiking, swimming or cycling, or through 'physical culture', that is, body-building. In Europe and America the pioneering bodybuilder Eugene Sandow promoted himself effectively as a model of physical perfection rather than as an exemplar of brute strength, and it was through photography that Sandow got his message across. His image appeared on millions of *cartes de visite*, larger-format cabinet cards, and cigarette cards.

Physical culture would take particular hold in France, and some of the credit was owed to photography. In the 1880s, the entrepreneur Edmond Desbonnet introduced his own highly effective method of developing both male and female physiques, proving the efficacy of his method with before-and-after photographs of his graduates (279) and photographs of his own well-muscled physique (171). He also hung photographs of famous athletes on the walls of his many salons around the country. Some of these were remarkably accomplished, anticipating the minimalist male nudes of the next century.

Although the static portrait remained the standard format of the sports photograph well into the twentieth century, the introduction of instantaneous photography in the 1880s signalled new possibilities. The development of the hand-held Kodak camera allowed the amateur to record athletic activities outdoors – a willingness to risk the lives of one's subjects was the only additional requirement (179). But there is little of exceptional quality in sports photography until the 1930s, by which time camera technology was up to the task.

It is to an amateur that we owe some of the most marvellous early-twentieth-century sports imagery. Jacques-Henri Lartigue was only a child when he began to document the antics of his family and friends in France during the Belle Epoque, but he quickly mastered the art of recording bodies jumping, falling, tripping and generally exhibiting *joie de vivre*. When as a young man he came across professional athletes the lessons of his early years stood him in good stead. His portrait-in-motion of the champion Géo André in training for the 1924 Olympics is an early masterpiece of the genre (185); the background of empty stands makes the viewer feel that he or she is a privileged observer of a behind-the-scenes event, and the rising form of the athlete, so evidently in control, suggests a coolly anticipated triumph.

With the German photographer Leni Riefenstahl, sports imagery rose to new aesthetic heights. Commissioned by Joseph Goebbels, she brought her considerable visual and organizational skills to bear on both photographing and filming the 1936 Olympic Games. Although the film *Olympiad* has become an acknowledged classic, her book of photographs, *Schönheit im Olympischen Kampf*, no less spectacular in its own way, is less known. Sometimes Riefenstahl relied on poses modelled on the antique Greek ideal, faithful to Hitler's belief that modern Teutonic man was 'feeling closer to classical antiquity' than he had 'in possibly a thousand years' (287).[1] But far more original were her depictions of superbly athletic bodies soaring gracefully through the air and knifing effortlessly through the water (184). Riefenstahl applied certain devices characteristic of the new German photography – strong diagonals, tight croppings, and bird's-eye and worm's-eye views. No longer was the camera an earthbound witness; it took to the air and the water with the athletes.

Hitler's adoration of the Greek ideal had not prevented him from closing the nudist parks in 1933. Nudism was too freethinking an ideology to be accommodated within the Nazi ideal of regimented bodies in the service of the state. Photography had done much to promote the liberation of the body, and it was a staple of the many magazines devoted to the nudist movement. A common motif was the joyous leaping figure – youthful, supple, sun-worshipping and free of earthly care. Gerhard Riebicke's variation on the theme might well have taken as its title one of the names of the movement itself, *Lichtkleid* – 'dressed in light' (193). Herbert List also saw youthful male vigour as a marvellous gift, but it was close physical contact with the soil and sea of his beloved Greece that he celebrated, rather than blind worship of the Sun God (192).

For the Russian utopian artist/photographer El Lissitzky, prowess meant the body functioning as a dynamic component of a machine civilization (191). His unusual pictorial approach was characteristic of his attempts to substitute the representation of energy for the representation of matter and to find new ways of depicting space. Like his avant-garde artist colleagues, Lissitzky believed in embracing new materials and techniques and would probably have approved of the 1951 Bulova Phototimer image of a track meet winner, with its wholly unintentional but beautifully expressive transformation of man into bird (190).

British photojournalist George Rodger, who travelled extensively in Uganda, Tanganyika, the Sudan and Southern Africa after the Second World War photographing tribal life, saw strength and beauty in a Nuba 'bracelet fighter' of the village of Kao challenging an opponent from the neighbouring village of Nyaro in a ritual display of prowess (183). For American photojournalist Ken Heyman, who also worked in Africa, an impressive physique was best displayed hard at work (187).

The professional sports photographer did not come into being until after the Second World War. Before then, press photographers were expected to cover athletic events along with everything else – a flood or fire in the morning, perhaps, 'the strongest boy in New York' or 'an eight-year-old child dancer and elocutionist' in the afternoon (177, 178).

The postwar breed of specialist was required to know his sport as well as his craft in order to pinpoint the critical moment of a race or fight, such as a knock-out blow (189), though often in sports imagery it is an unintended visual effect which catches our interest – an awkward 'dance' of two tennis players (197) or the 'synthesis' of two wrestlers' bodies into one (188).

Where we find imagery in which these kinds of correspondences are intended, however, it is usually in the archives of wholly independent photographers whose allegiance is to their own vision. Leon Levinstein's handball jitterbug or Helen Levitt's basketball ballet are the happy consequences of snap reflexes and keen eyes for chance occurrences (198, 199). Aaron Siskind on the other hand actually *sent* bodies on existential journeys in his 1950s series, *The Pleasures and Terrors of Levitation*, suggesting that the physical thrills bodies invariably seek are fraught with unknown psychological perils (202).

Walery
Edmond Desbonnet c. 1885
Gelatin silver print

We are used to athletes filling the frame, overpowering us with their presence, but in her baseball photographs U.S. photographer Danielle Weil has taken the fan's more distant view, preferring to cast the players as heroic Lilliputians, performing their arabesques on a vast geometric canvas. In *The Delivery*, a pitcher unleashes the forces that drive the game (194). Weil restored the sense of grace which had been wrung out of baseball by the media's hunger for close-ups. Fashion photographer Aldo Rossi also proves that high drama can be crafted with tiny forms (195). His unusual vantage point sends diver Mary Ellen Clark hurtling like a spacecraft towards a mysterious planet.

Like sports photography, dance photography is essentially a twentieth-century practice. In the early years there were no specialized dance photographers and attempts to document live performance were doomed to failure. Not until the 1930s was camera, film and lighting technology up to the task of producing dance photographs in which the figures were not blurred. Ironically, it was after the problem was solved, with the strobe, and dancers could be frozen in mid-air, that the blur reappeared as an aesthetic device.

Witzel Studio, Los Angeles
Ted Shawn in *Gnossiene* 1919
Gelatin silver print

Imogen Cunningham
Martha Graham performing privately for the camera 1931
Gelatin silver print

Inevitably the finest work in dance photography has been accomplished by photographers who have refused to accept the handmaiden status of their medium *vis-à-vis* dance, and have insisted on an equal partnership. Such mutual respect for what critic Elisabeth McCausland called the 'twin arts of dance and photography' sparked an afternoon of experiment by Martha Graham and Imogen Cunningham in which the dancer uncharacteristically performed partially nude (*above*).[2] There is an uninhibited quality to Cunningham's photographs, suggesting that the two artists were responding creatively to each other.

Traditionally, one way round the technical limitations of dance photography has been to photograph outdoors, where sufficient light for quick exposures is not a problem. At the end of the nineteenth century this outdoors motif **173**

W. G. Hill
The Combat 1918
Carbon print

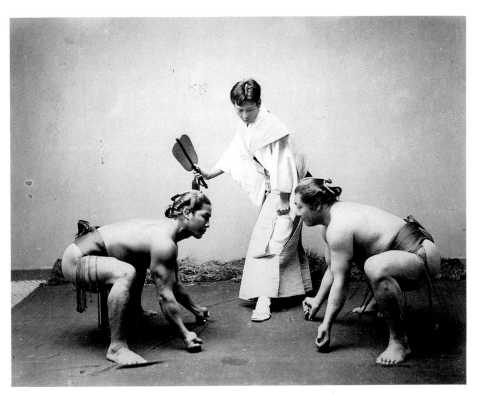

Anonymous
Untitled c. 1870
Albumen print

corresponded to a desire on the part of certain dancers to commune with the natural world, thus healing the rift that was seen to have opened between nature and the human soul. Isadora Duncan, Loie Fuller, Ruth St Denis and a host of acolytes pranced barefoot by the sea, heads thrown back and arms ecstatically extended.

Today these earnest pictures appear naive, if endearing. It might seem strange, therefore, that the genre has been revitalized by a photographer who has chosen to record the work of a number of choreographers known for their hard-nosed, city-based art. However, this very ambivalence has invested the work of Philip Trager with a certain psychological tension (203). Far from finding contact with Mother Earth a comforting experience, Trager's thoroughly post-modern protagonists greet it with trepidation. **175**

S. M. Poppoff
Bulgarian Contortionist c. 1890
Albumen print

That there is a good deal of life left in the studio tradition of dance photography is proven by the electrifying imagery of New York photographer Lois Greenfield. For more than twenty years the stars and hopefuls of the modern and postmodern dance world have catapulted themselves across her surprisingly diminutive studio, later to see their likenesses rising, floating and falling weightlessly in seemingly infinite space (205).

But for all her contributions to the dance world, it is photography of the body in motion that remains Greenfield's passion. Dance is her vehicle, or as she puts it, 'my landscape'.[3] She needs the bodies of dancers rather than ordinary bodies because of their physical accomplishment, their ability to previsualize themselves in space, to chart their trajectories and land with pinpoint accuracy. But she will not pose them. Instead, telling them to 'leave their choreography at the door,' she gets them dancing and, as critic Deborah Jowitt puts it, 'snatches the image out of a field of motion'.[4] □

176

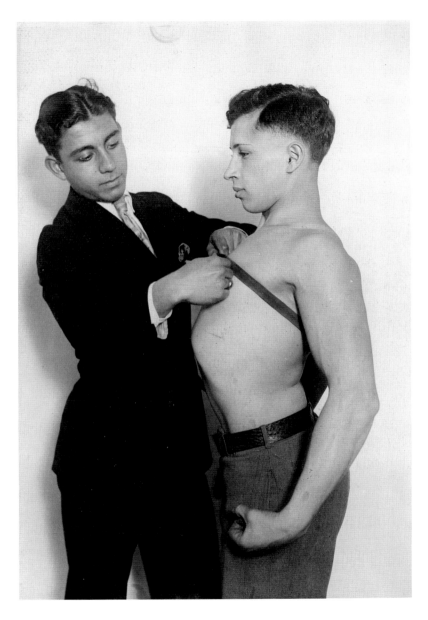

Anonymous
The Strongest Boy in New York: Harry Luft 1926
Gelatin silver print

Anonymous
Eight-year-old Dancer and Elocutionist n.d.
Gelatin silver print

George Fiske
Clowning on Observation Point, Yosemite Valley c. 1905
Gelatin silver print

178

National Commercial Photo. Co., Chicago
Champion Johnny Meyers Putting the Finishing Grip on His Foe, the Body Scissors and the Deep Half-Nelson n.d.
Gelatin silver print

Mary Ellen Mark
Indian Circus 1989
Gelatin silver print

Anonymous
Schoolboy Weightlifting Prodigy 1931
Gelatin silver print

George Rodger
The Challenger 1949
Gelatin silver print

Leni Riefenstahl
The Winning High-Diver Dorothy Poynton-Hill, U.S.A. 1936
Gelatin silver print

Jacques-Henri Lartigue
Paris: Stade de Colombes, le grand champion
Géo André s'entraine pour les Olympiques
(Paris: Stade de Colombes, the Grand Champion Géo André
in Training for the Olympics) 1924
Gelatin silver print

René-Jacques
Illustration for 'Les Olympiques' by Henri de Montherlant 1948
Gelatin silver print

Ken Heyman
Railsplitter, Lagos, Nigeria 1972
Gelatin silver print

Anonymous
When Greek Meets Greek 1931
Gelatin silver print

Herb Scharfman
Rocky Marciano K.O.'s Jersey Joe Walcott 1952
Gelatin silver print

El Lissitzky
Footballer c. 1926
Gelatin silver print from collage

Bulova Phototimer photo
*James Gehrdes Winning the 60-Yard High
Hurdles at the New York Athletic Club
Meet, February 1951*
Gelatin silver print

191

Herbert List
Untitled c. 1930
Gelatin silver print

Gerhard Riebicke
Leaping Man c. 1930
Half-tone reproduction

Danielle Weil
The Delivery 1990
Gelatin silver print

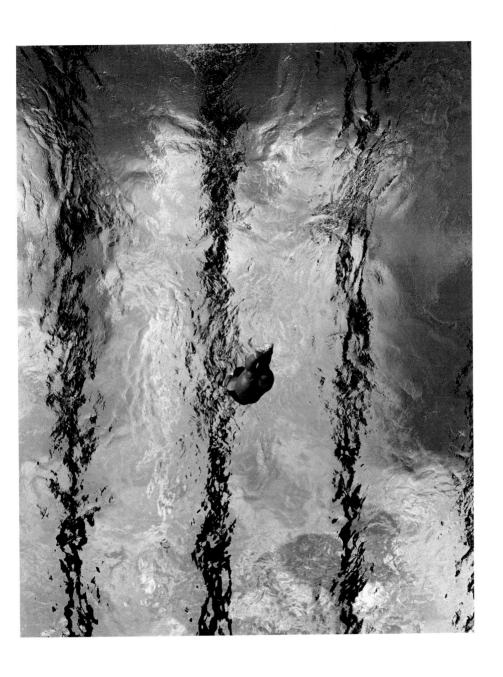

Aldo Rossi
Mary Ellen Clark, U.S. Olympic Diver, Hall of Fame Pool, Fort Lauderdale, Florida 1993
Gelatin silver print

Anonymous
Marian Fitting in Training, Pasadena Athletic Club n.d.
Gelatin silver print

Anonymous
Gertrude (Gorgeous Gussy) Moran and Mrs Pat Todd, of La Jolla, California, at Wimbledon 1956
Gelatin silver print

Leon Levinstein
Handball Players c. 1965
Gelatin silver print

Helen Levitt
Brooklyn 1982
Gelatin silver print

Robert Mapplethorpe
Lisa Lyon 1982
Gelatin silver print

Western Photography Guild
Wrestlers c. 1940
Gelatin silver print

Aaron Siskind
The Pleasures and Terrors of Levitation 1956
Gelatin silver print

Philip Trager
Arthur Aviles 1992
Gelatin silver print

Anonymous
Serge Lifar n.d.
Gelatin silver print

Lois Greenfield
Andrew Pacho and Kim Anthony of the ANTIGRAVITY Dance Company 1992
Gelatin silver print

EROS

. . . a thousand hungry eyes are bending over the peepholes of the
stereoscope as though they were the attic windows of the infinite.
The love of pornography, which is no less deeply rooted in the natural
heart of man than love of himself, was not to let slip so fine an
opportunity of self-satisfaction. And do not imagine that it was only
children on their way back from school who took pleasure in these
follies; everyone was infatuated with them.

CHARLES BAUDELAIRE
'The Modern Public and Photography', 1859

Is there such a thing as an erotic image or is eroticism purely a function of the gaze? We know that individuals respond differently to sexually explicit material and that all kinds of factors, apart from sexual orientation, influence that response – age, experience, libido, moral values, even fashions and diverse cultural forces. What one person sees as sensuous and beautiful, the next sees as prurient and obscene.

One way of defining whether or not an image is erotic might be to ask if it was intended as such. From the earliest days of photography certain entrepreneurs recognized that its unmatched realism offered the voyeur a new level of sexual thrill. The makers of daguerreotypes were quick to respond with titillating imagery for their well-heeled clients. Explicit sexual content with vivid depictions of perverse practices was not always what was wanted; suggestion and mood were highly valued and sometimes pains were taken to devise images reminiscent of Baroque and Rococo painting (211).

Paris was the centre of the flourishing trade, and items could be bought, though not displayed, at opticians' shops and in the luxury brothels. A studio

Erwin Blumenfeld
Nude under Wet Silk, Paris 1937
Gelatin silver print

which specialized in erotica usually employed no more than half a dozen models and made do with the very simplest of props – a divan, a surfeit of rich fabric, and, for the model herself, a garland of flowers and a few pieces of jewelry. A final seductive touch was the hand-colouring of the daguerreotype, with particular attention given to the flesh tones. The introduction of a stereo format in the 1850s added yet another voyeuristic dimension. For several decades after the medium as a whole had fallen into disuse, erotic daguerreotypes would continue to flourish.

Being one-of-a-kind objects, daguerreotypes had a restricted circulation. Photographic erotica would become a mass-market phenomenon only in the 1850s with the introduction of the negative/positive process, which allowed unlimited numbers of copies of any image. By all accounts the development of this market was rapid and exponential. The press of the period constantly reported seizures of huge troves of 'indecent' materials; the numbers given were often in excess of 100,000.

The new market posed problems for photographers and dealers, who now had to steer clear of the law and public condemnation without forgoing the enormous profits. Explicit pornography presented no real difficulty because it remained underground (218). The chief problem was with the tamer variety, in which 'women exposed their legs while lacing their boots' or 'reclined on couches in exciting postures.'[1] Here the law was unclear. Should such material be seized, it might, or might not, ruin a dealer and his photographer/suppliers. The moral and legal muddle was reflected in many indignant newspaper and magazine articles:

There is hardly a street in London which does not contain shops in which photographs, and especially stereoscopic photographs, are exposed for sale, *which are certainly not positively indecent*, but which *it is equally clear are expressly intended* for the gratification of that pruriency which parliament tried to deprive of its coarser stimulus . . . To our mind there is something positively sacrilegious in the idea of prostituting the light of heaven to such debasing purposes (Author's italics).[2]

Few late-nineteenth-century viewers would have had any complaint about the decorous Neoclassical nudes made by partners Louis Amadée Mantes and Edmond Goldschmidt (213), so close in style to those of William Bouguereau

PRISES ..... AU DAGUERRÉOTYPE
_ Ah !..... Clarisse ..... vois donc cette grande machine ..... on dirait qu'il y a un œil qui nous regarde !.....

' Ah . . . Clarisse . . . look at that big machine . . . I could swear
it was looking at us.' c. 1845
Lithograph

and Lawrence Alma-Tadema. Nor would Eugène Durieu's nudes, which conformed to accepted painterly conventions, be likely to cause offence (214).

However, there would have been no question as to the prurience of *England* (218), or the lasciviousness of the young girl's pose in the anonymous photograph on page 220. Less certain is the reception F.-J. Moulin's flirtatious *L'Odalisque et son esclave* would have had in polite society (215). Like the freespirited nudes of Albert Penot (216, 217), it was probably produced for, or even commissioned by, a wealthy customer.

Moulin's exotic fantasy was typical of many licentious photographs of the period. The harem was an enduring theme (219), as was the carnal black African **209** woman, whether giving herself freely to her European masters or being taken by force (248, 261). The German photographer Guglielmo Plüschow provided an unusual variation on the interracial theme by depicting a voluptuous white woman about to be ravished by a black African Pan (225).

For the homosexual clientele, the Mediterranean was a particularly erogenous zone. Young Italian males were thought to mature sexually several years before boys in the North, and their sexual proclivities were said to be notoriously 'catholic'. Most importantly, Italian society was tolerant of temporary liaisons between young boys and older men. The German photographer Baron Wilhelm von Gloeden mined this territory, directing his young Sicilian charges in an erotic theatre of the antique (212, 223). Plüschow and Vincenzo Galdi (222) sometimes visited Von Gloeden's secluded Taormina villa, and posed his young charges (who occasionally included adolescent girls) in an equally provocative manner.

The distinction between a legitimately sensual image and a blatantly pornographic one remained a grey and troublesome area in the nineteenth century and many photographers with a commercial interest in sexually stimulating imagery exploited the confusion. Even the anatomical photographs made as aids for artists could find their way into the hands of unscrupulous dealers. In short, the stage was set for similar twentieth-century patterns.

With the introduction of the halftone printing plate in the 1890s, erotic photographs began to appear in books, magazines, calendars and postcards. At first production was French, but a shift in attitudes to the body as a consequence of the First World War led to more widespread manufacture and consumption in Europe and America. This printed genre of nude was a curiously de-sexed creature: no sexual organs, no pubic hair, often no nipples and sometimes no navel. Expressions were coy, and captions, when they appeared, were filled with *double entendres*. Book titles invoked biblical myths to win a measure of respectability; typical were *Eves without Leaves* and *Adam's Fifth Rib*.

Influential fashion magazines such as *Vogue* and *Harper's Bazaar* showed the body with increasing daring and creativity. James Abbe thrilled readers with his sensual nude studies of stage and film stars (226), and if his risqué backstage views of the Folies-Bergère were a little too forthright for American publications, their European counterparts had no such misgivings (227).

Anonymous
Nude study of two female figures 1855
Daguerreotype

One of the most inventive of the new breed of professional fashion photographers in America was the German émigré Erwin Blumenfeld. Fashion and beauty assignments were often excuses for him to indulge his passion for erotic themes, and he put his wide-ranging knowledge of painting and sculpture to good use. He noted of Cranach the Elder's nudes that 'their insolent beauty [is] all the more naked for their transparent veils' (207).[3]

From the 1940s and 1950s on, *Adonis, Tomorrow's Man* and other homoerotic magazines offered their clients a hybrid male image – part nineteenth-century classical figure study, part bodybuilder ideal, part Hollywood 'pin-up'. They drew their 'physique photography' from competing studios – Spartan, Athletic Model Guild, Bruce of Los Angeles and Western >>>

Wilhelm von Gloeden
Untitled c. 1890
Albumen print

Louis Amédée Mantes and Edmond Goldschmidt
The Lily Pool c. 1895-1905
Original: colour diapositive on glass

Photography Guild (233-35). Original photographs could also be ordered from the studios, and it was this mail-order activity, rather than the magazines, which kept the rivals in business. The Athletic Model Guild (despite its name the sole property of Robert Mizer) churned out on average 20,000 images a year. Prints were usually small enough (4 x 5 inches) to pass discreetly through the mail. As blatant sexual activity was illegal, the erotic had to be suggested rather than shown, and motifs such as wrestling were a means of legitimizing physical intimacy. However, the oiled bodies left no doubt that these were objects of desire.[4]

For heterosexual males of the 1950s, an essential ingredient of the popular pin-up was coyness. Curvaceous blondes were posed outdoors surrounded by the new toys of middle-class affluence – swimming pools, deckchairs, sports equipment, etc. (229). The awkwardness of their poses was deliberate – it was meant to suggest that their real talents lay in bed. Indoors,the bubble bath was second only to the rumpled sheet in pin-up iconography (228).

Eugène Durieu
Untitled c. 1853
Salt print

François-Jacques Moulin
L'Odalisque et son esclave (*Odalisque and Her Slave*) 1853
Albumen print

From the 1950s on the commercial market for such nudes increased enormously, and calendars, books and magazines specializing in the genre routinely sold in their millions. Publications such as *Playboy* and *Penthouse* became fixtures of male heterosexual culture. For the most part the treatment of these nudes rapidly became formulaic and banal; legal restraints and social taboos left little opportunity for inventiveness. Nor has the gradual easing of taboos over the decade resulted in any furthering of the aesthetic. This genre is probably best thought of as eroticized folk art.

By contrast, fine art photographers (that is, those who use the medium as one of personal expression) have handled the subject of eroticism with subtlety and daring. Sometimes their representation of sexual activity is detached and ironic. Frank Horvat's view of a striptease, for example, is distanced and cool: it includes the spectators, suggesting that his subject is, in contemporary parlance, the power of the male gaze (231). George Zimbel, on the other hand, is a front-row voyeur (230). On occasion the feeling of sexuality in a photographer's work can **215**

Albert Penot
Untitled c. 1900
Albumen print

be overpowering. Pierre Molinier's intertwined female limbs indicate an
obsession as strong as that of his Surrealist predecessor Hans Bellmer (232). For
Molinier this obsession had to do with taking on a female identity, and in much
of his imagery the fetishistic bouquets of limbs are his own. A poetic eroticism,
entirely devoid of licentiousness, suffuses the work of Ralph Gibson and Lucien
Clergue (236, 237), though their work differs considerably. Clergue has always
felt the need to underline the traditional association of women's bodies with
nature: his model's voluptuous curves mirror ripples in the sand, rock pools and
waves. For Gibson a woman's erotic power stems also from the way her body is
groomed, dressed and adorned. His fragmentary perspective is not just a formal
device – a means of indulging his love of abstraction – it is also a way of
withholding, or holding back, and thereby deepening the sense of mystery. If
any single factor separates the true eroticist from the pornographer, it is this. □   **217**

Anonymous
England 1865
Albumen print

Albert
L'Algérie pittoresque, Mauresque (Picturesque, Moorish Algeria) c. 1900
Albumen print

219

Anonymous
Untitled 1890s
Albumen print

Anonymous
Untitled c. 1920
Gelatin silver print

221

Vincenzo Galdi
Girl, Italy c. 1900
Albumen print

Wilhelm von Gloeden
Untitled c. 1890
Albumen print

223

Anonymous (French)
Boy Kissing Girl c. 1880
Albumen print

Guglielmo Plüschow
Black and White Nudes c. 1890
Albumen print

James Abbe, Sr
Bessie Love in Paris Studio 1928
Gelatin silver print

James Abbe, Sr
Backstage at the Folies-Bergère 1924
Gelatin silver print

Anonymous
Untitled *c.* 1950
Gelatin silver print

Anonymous
Untitled 1950s
Gelatin silver print

Frank Horvat
Strip-tease 1955-57
Gelatin silver print

George S. Zimbel
Chelo, Bourbon Street, New Orleans 1955
Gelatin silver print

Pierre Molinier
Skin d'Amourdo 1970s
Gelatin silver print

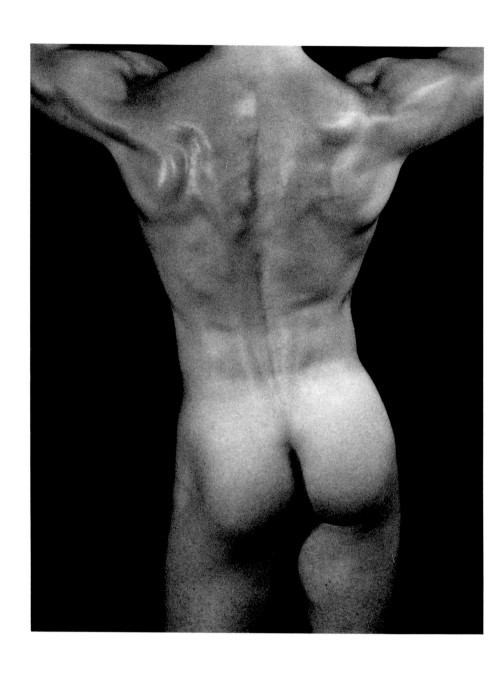

Western Photography Guild
Untitled c. 1940s
Gelatin silver print

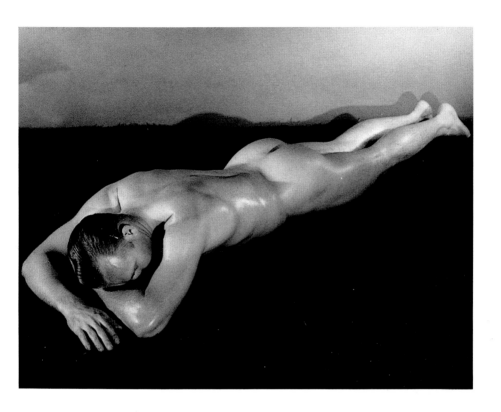

Athletic Model Guild
Untitled c. 1940s
Gelatin silver print

Lucien Clergue
Italy 1993
Gelatin silver print

Ralph Gibson
Paris 1986
Gelatin silver print

237

ESTRANGEMENT

Mankind which in Homer's time was an object of contemplation for the Olympic gods, now is one for itself. Its self-alienation has reached such a degree that it can experience its own destruction as an aesthetic pleasure of the first order.

WALTER BENJAMIN, *Illuminations*, 1936

The stream of genetic knowledge which began to flow in the 1970s has now reached the proportions of a deluge; within our lifetimes we can expect to see the full genetic blueprint of the human body. The implications – moral and ethical, social and political, are bewildering. Human beings are gradually being given the tools to alter the natural order, to reinvent themselves. There are already reports of parents aborting foetuses which do not conform to the desired genetic profile, and talk about 'designer babies' and 'clones' is not merely speculative. Not surprisingly, a certain alienation or estrangement is concomitant with these new realities.

'The body' that we read or hear about in the news is necessarily a generalized construct, an abstraction. But each of us remains firmly enveloped in a specific body, subject to its own idiosyncratic dynamics, its strengths and weaknesses. There may be a tantalizing future for the universal body – of youth and vitality restored to the aged, of vastly extended lifespans, of a range of improvements hitherto relegated to the realm of science fiction – but ultimately each person has to confront his or her own corporeal reality. This discrepancy must always be a source of great anxiety for the individual, because at its root is a certain

238   knowledge of eventual death.

Photography has undoubtedly improved our physical and mental well-being. As a tool of science and medicine its contributions are beyond dispute, and as an art form it has enriched our understanding of the body in less quantifiable but no less significant ways. Not only have photographs convinced us of the profound aesthetic pleasures to be gained from contemplation of the body; they have also forced us to confront the darker sides of our natures, the fears and irrationalities that may drive us ultimately to deprive and abuse the bodies of others.

Photographers of war and its horrific aftermath are among those who have not been afraid to hold a mirror to these negative forces (266, 267). Shomei Tomatsu's image of a Hiroshima victim's hideous scar is a reminder of the twentieth century's appetite for killing on a grand scale. Every living person looking at this image must realize that she/he too, in the atomic age, is – in Paul Virilio's words – 'a human negative',[1] waiting to be processed. There is no doubt that we are better informed about the human consequences of wars, famines and all natural and man-made catastrophes as a result of ubiquitous photographic imagery, although, as Walter Benjamin suggests, rather than sensitizing us it may have been one of the forces contributing to quite the opposite effect, leaving us passive and demoralized.

We often look away when confronted with imagery of the sick, the deformed, the dead and dying, but in the nineteenth century there was a brisk trade in such photographs of 'the other'; the circus freak, the bearded lady, Siamese twins, and so forth were popular subjects to be collected and traded (244-47, 262-63).

To the extent that we worry about exploitation of bodies which do not conform to the norm or suffer from some affliction, our reticence is humane; but to the extent that we refuse to confront the human condition, it is pathological. A number of contemporary photographers have taken up the subject of death and disease in order to force such a confrontation.

Diane Michener's images of turn-of-the-century babies preserved in bottles speak of lives which sparked only briefly before being extinguished (270, 271). Yet we cannot fail to observe that these small creatures were human beings, capable of expression and gesture. Michener's respectful, even loving treatment gives them a life in the 'imaginary' which they were cruelly denied in the material world.

239

Jeffrey Silverthorne's study of the corpse of a young woman after autopsy is poignant to the point of pain (268). This is partly because the position of her limbs and head evoke a classic nude. So peaceful is the facial expression, so 'alive' the presence, that we struggle against the incontestable evidence provided by the stitches. We are used to seeing in the newspaper images of violent death, ugly and repellent, but this is a reminder of another of its faces, just as incomprehensible, perhaps, but undeniably serene and beautiful.

Interestingly, photography of the dead has not always been a perilous subject. In its early years it was one of the medium's widespread applications. Old people, for whom photography had arrived too late to commemorate the significant moments of their lives, made careful arrangements to have it record their final passage. Dead babies were another popular subject. Although to our thinking there is something of the macabre in this practice, people in the nineteenth century seemed to find much solace in it, as they did also in the so-called spirit photograph, a portrait of a widow or widower with an image of the dearly departed (manufactured by double-exposure) hovering reassuringly over the shoulder.

Ironically, it is in photographs of the living that we detect an early hint of estrangement. By 1880 photographs commemorating *rites de passage* and other significant family occasions were common household treasures. But these vivid mementoes had an unanticipated effect, as if the bright light photography shone on the past brought that past into uncomfortably sharp focus. We can detect the beginnings of this unease in an account from the *Photographic News* in 1880:

> An era has set in which may be fitly termed *an era of regrets*. We find, it is true, that photographs fade, but not so quickly, alas, as the friends and acquaintances they represent. Grown up men and women look curiously at their baby photographs, and grandfather and grandmother turn back the pages with trembling hands to see themselves in wedding garments and muse on the times of years ago . . .
>
> After a while we shall grow accustomed *to the hard truths the camera teaches us*, but the present generation is the first to appreciate them to the full. That life is but a span is illustrated in every family album in the kingdom, and the adage was never so vividly and frequently brought home to us as in these days of photography (Author's italics).[2]

T. Andrew
Fijian Cannibals c. 1890
Albumen print

This ambivalent response may help to explain the change in attitude towards the family album, which went from being in its early days a compendium of novelties, shown freely and enthusiastically to visitors, to something of a sacred trust, fitted with lock and key. Noted the *News*, 'It is treated with a reverence that day to day becomes more marked.'[3]

Photography brought with it a new awareness of self-image, but at a cost – the separation of the self from the body. This is reflected in accounts of people preparing themselves for encounters with the camera:

> Next to getting married, we think there is more talk and more fussing 'gone through with' to get one's self ready to have a photograph made than for anything else. This is perfectly legitimate, because one desires to look well, especially when one is to be handed round, criticized and admired among his friends, and preserved for posterity.[4]

Anonymous
Deformed foot, China c. 1870
Albumen print

Nadar (Gaspard-Félix Tournachon)
Hermaphrodite 1861
Albumen print

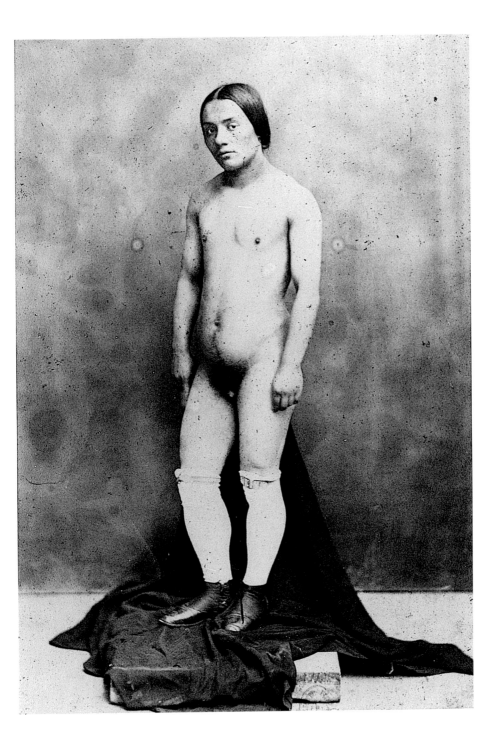

Anonymous
James Morris, Elastic Skin Man c. 1890
Albumen print

Anonymous
*A Filipino Freak of Seven or
Eight Years Old Having an
Extra Pair of Legs Protruding
from the Pelvis* c. 1900
Gelatin silver print

Anonymous (French)
Untitled c. 1890
Albumen print

 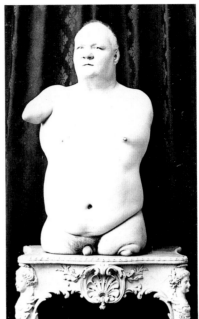

The implications of this awareness – that a self-image could be constructed for the camera more or less independently of the physical body – would not be fully apparent for one hundred years or more, but today it is commonplace reality for mass-media entertainers, who truly exist in a disembodied ether.

Sometimes a photographer provides us with a symbol of our own estrangement, as Antonin Kratochvil does in his remarkable image of a man of almost incomprehensible obesity lying in his lair at a Florida sideshow (269). We gaze at this sea of flesh spellbound, before being caught up short by a mirror image of our alter egos, in the window, gawping and incredulous.

It would be wrong to characterize or dismiss the photographic art as inherently (or at least, merely) voyeuristic. Sometimes a subject will willingly collaborate with a photographer in order to communicate an aspect of self, or self-expression, as Stefan Richter's *David* does, albeit ambivalently (265). Richter believes that his 'gentle intrusions' are respectful to the individual and enlightening to the viewer, revealing a dimension of cultural *practice* normally shrouded in secrecy.[5] **245**

PRINCESS WEE WEE

#3

© RIDENOUR PHILA

(left) Charles E. Ridenour
*Princess Wee Wee, The Smallest Perfectly Formed Little Woman in the World,
Age 23, Weight 12 Pounds, Height 25 Inches, May 20, 1915*
Postcard

Anonymous
The Human Skeleton Weds the Fat Lady 1924
Stereograph

But we must be careful to distinguish between this kind of photography – mediated by compassion and respect for the subject, lifting the veil on the hidden and perverse in order to engender understanding – and other forms which exploit different and distant bodies and contribute to the estrangement of one body from another. Photography is often employed to deceive, to exacerbate anxieties and to reinforce stereotypes and prejudices. T. Andrew's late-nineteenth-century theatrical depiction of supposed Fijian cannibals played into the hands of missionaries and colonialists who wanted evidence that distant tribal peoples were morally inferior, and therefore justifiably subject to the controls of more civilized peoples (241).

Much of the early photography of 'exotic' peoples seems to have been inspired by lust as well as fear, or at least by a fascination with their relative nakedness. In the minds of many European photographers and their male clients, black **247**

(opposite) Luigi Naretti
Mesdames (Eritrea) c. 1885
Albumen print

Attributed to Nuredin & Levin
Scenes and Types; Arabian Woman with the Yashmak c. 1880
Modern gelatin silver print

African women were primarily objects of desire, deeply carnal creatures, amoral and yielding to the superior power of the white, like the Dark Continent itself (*left*). Arab women, too, were objectified in erotic terms (*above*) and the veil seems to have been a particularly exciting piece of clothing. 'These veiled women are not only an embarrassing enigma to the photographer, but an outright attack on him,' writes Malek Alloula on the colonial harem, '. . . this womanly gaze is a little like the eye of the camera, like the photographic lens that takes aim at everything.'[6] □

249

Willoughby Wallace Hooper
Starving Indians, Madras (South India) 1876
Albumen print

Felice Beato
*Crucifixion of the Male Servant Sokichi Who Killed the Son of His Boss
and Was Therefore Crucified. He Was 25 Years Old.* 1865-68
Albumen print

Attributed to Alinari Brothers
Cemetero dei Cappuccini, Roma (Cemetery of the Cappuccini, Rome) c. 1870
Albumen print

Giorgio Sommer
Impression of the Body of a Woman Found in Pompeii c. 1865
Albumen print

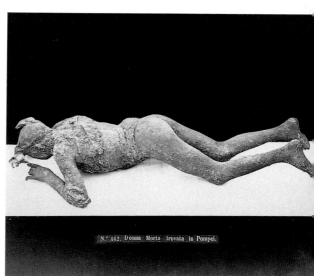

N.° 462. Donna Morta trovata in Pompei.

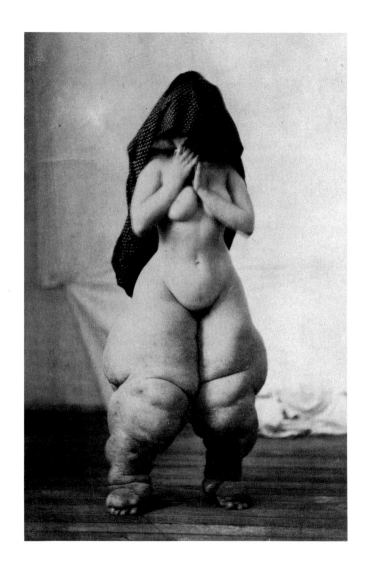

O. G. Mason
Veiled Lady (Elephantiasis due to Scarlet Fever) 1878
Artotype (Heliotype)

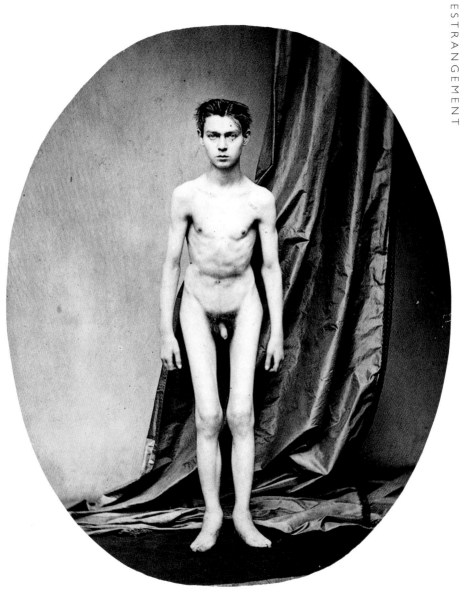

L. Haase
Patient of Dr Hermann Wolff Berend, with orthopaedic condition c. 1864
Albumen print

Anonymous
Lipoma Ossifying c. 1910
Lantern slide

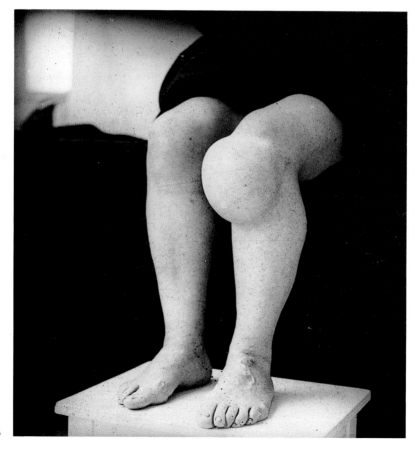

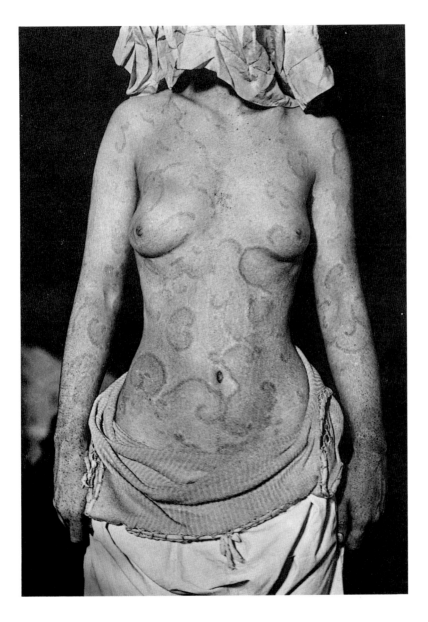

Henry G. Piffard
The Paisley Lady (Erythema Annulare) c. 1891
Artotype (Heliotype)

Anonymous
Wens: Malignant c. 1910
Lantern slide

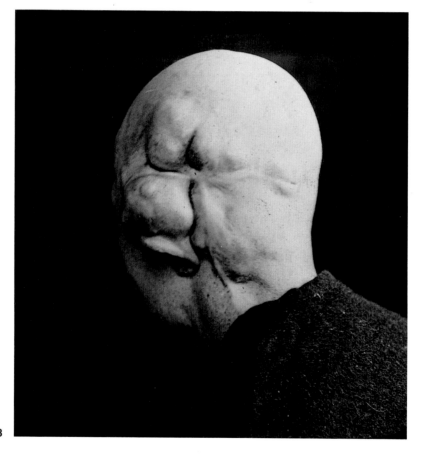

Anonymous
Congenital Tumour Sterno Mastoid c. 1910
Lantern slide

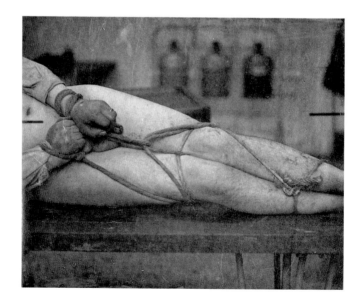

Anonymous
Affaire du bureau de poste à Strasbourg les 28/29 Décembre 1920. Le facteur
(*The Strasbourg Post Office Affair, 28/29 December 1920. The Postman*) (detail) 1920
Gelatin silver print

260

Lehnert & Landrock
Esclave attachée, Tunisia (Bound Slave, Tunisia) c. 1900
Arrowroot/Gelatin gold bromide

Progress Studio
The Hilton Siamese Twins of Texas 1925
Gelatin silver prints

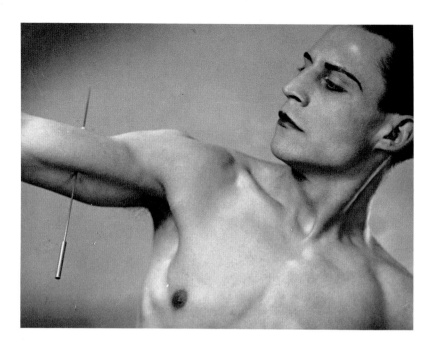

Anonymous
Untitled c. 1925-30
Gelatin silver print

Stefan Richter
David, Amsterdam 1989
From original colour transparency

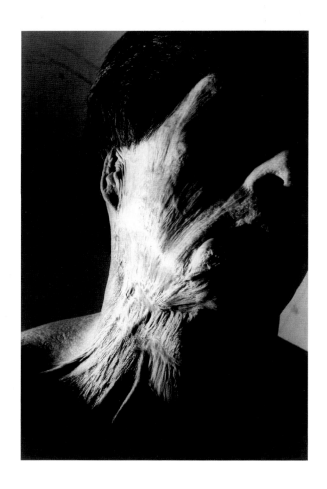

Shomei Tomatsu
From the *Nagasaki* series n.d.
Gelatin silver print

Lee Miller
Prisoners with Human Remains, Buchenwald 1945
Gelatin silver print

Jeffrey Silverthorne
The Woman Who Died in Her Sleep 1972
Gelatin silver print

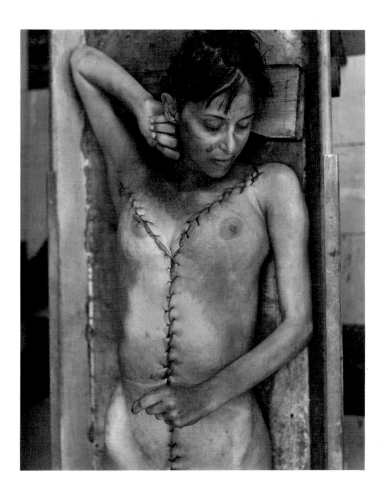

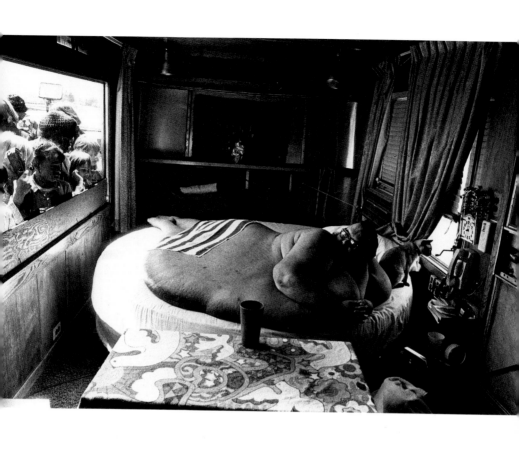

Antonin Kratochvil
Florida Sideshow 1975
Gelatin silver print

269

Diana Michener
F.56, Sympus 1987
Gelatin silver print

Diana Michener
F.69, Cephalo-Toracopagus 1987
Gelatin silver print

271

IDOLS

As things are going, the community will soon be divided, roughly, into two classes – viz, that one which comprises the individuals who, on some ground, are considered eligible to have their photos taken, and that much more numerous one which is made up of all the people eager, on all possible occasions, to take them.

The Photographic News, 16 March 1889

Our culture holds the 'body beautiful' in great esteem. 'Models', we call the templates of physical perfection which gaze at us seductively from all sides. These are the true idols of our age, representing beauty, vitality, health, youth, even freedom. Should this celebration of bodily ideals be seen as a welcome shift from the repression of physicality that has characterized so many periods in the past? Or is the picture in fact far less rosy?

Today the cult of physical perfection often leads to obsession and neurosis. The rising incidence of the eating disorders anorexia and bulimia and the increasingly widespread recourse to cosmetic surgery as a means of enhancing beauty and cheating the aging process suggest a dark side to the quest for bodily perfection. 'In terms of how we feel about ourselves physically', observes Naomi Wolf of modern women, 'we may actually be worse off than our unliberated grandmothers.'[1] Nor are men of today free of anxieties relating to their supposed physical shortcomings.

The seeds of these anxieties are often sown by photography, most significantly by advertising imagery, which encourages us to compare our own imperfect

Anonymous
Miss Swim *c.* 1905
Gelatin silver print

Miss Swim

bodies with the idealized forms of others. The fact that these idealized body images bear little relation to reality but have been carefully fabricated by photographers in collusion with stylists, make-up artists, fashion and beauty editors, retouchers and printers generally passes unnoticed. Photography of this kind is so persuasive that it is taken as absolute proof of the efficacy of this or that product, regimen or 'lifestyle'. The 'before-and-after' photographic comparison remains a staple advertising technique one hundred years after it was first used (279).

In the very early days of photography all that was required of a photograph was that it should register a true likeness, as close as possible to a mirror image. When portraits became commonplace, however, satisfaction with the simple mirror image wore thin, and more idealized conceptions of the self became increasingly attractive. Because portraits were cheap and the sitter could purchase any number of copies, they were seen by more and more people, often people whom the sitter had never met or did not know – his or her relatives in distant lands and their friends, for example. The portrait functioned therefore as a kind of surrogate or ambassador for the self. In this sense it was more than a commemorative mark; it represented an extension of personal power – the power to influence the judgment and behaviour of others.

Then, as now, people wanted to project as commanding a self-image as possible and they made careful preparations for their encounters with the camera, taking advice on how to dress, pose and gesture from the popular manuals published at the time. By the 1860s photographers too had learned 'a great many things in the way of fixing up and beautifying the person with a view to having a picture made'.[2] Clients were dazzled by the elegant likenesses which stared back at them from increasingly elaborate matts and frames, from porcelain plates, expensive fabrics and other exotic supports. And, thanks to the skilful intervention of the retoucher, those faces were younger, more beautiful, more serene.

Celebrities demanded the same idealizing treatment, especially as they had grown accustomed to flattering depictions of themselves in lithographs and etchings. But in fact what the public of the time wanted in a photograph of a celebrity was the *un*idealized view, a likeness of a real person rather than a vision

274 of an ethereal god or goddess.   >>>

Ellis & Walery
Wooing, 'The Seldoms' at the London Pavilion 1907
Silver bromide print

275

Pesme
Jules Léotard c. 1860
Albumen print/*carte-de-visite*

Anonymous
One of the 'Deriaz' Brothers; The Desbonnet Method c. 1902
Modern silver print

Richard
The Atrium; The Desbonnet Method c. 1912
Modern silver print

Anonymous
Before and After, Or the Results of the Desbonnet Method c. 1908
Modern silver print

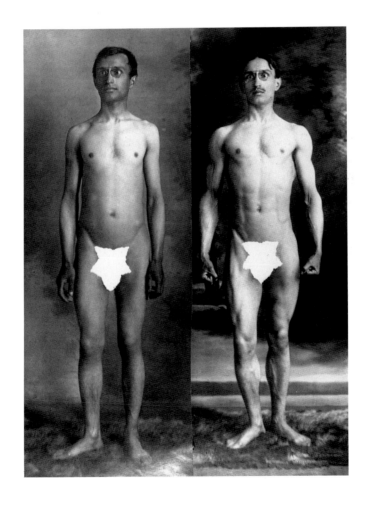

Anonymous
Bud Counts and His Mother Oiling His Body c. 1950
From Ektacolor print

Bruce of Los Angeles (Bruce Bellas)
Third Place, Jerry Boily of Vancouver, Muscle Beach, Venice, California c. 1957
Gelatin silver print

MUSCLE BEACH

The wildly popular celebrity *cartes de visite* of the 1860s, which were bought, exhibited and traded in their millions, allowed ordinary people to feel an unprecedented intimacy with famous figures. Such was their appeal that they could create a cult following for a person of even mediocre talent. Demand was high, price low, and images were churned out with little regard for any idealizing aesthetic.

Inevitably, however, the demand for realism was soon satisfied, and larger format photographs which allowed for more artful interpretation asserted their prominence. Even the little photographs of female beauties which were slipped into cigarette packages in the 1890s conformed to these idealizing tendencies. These new stars peeked coyly from their boudoirs, or posed in angelic robes and wings.

The enormous demand for photographs of beautiful women for various promotional schemes had the effect of creating a new kind of celebrity, one who was famous not for any particular talent or social attribute, but merely for being photogenic. The *Photographic News* called her a 'professional beauty', complaining that 'photography and society journals must share between them the onus of having invented such a purposeless creature.'[3]

These female idols had their male equivalents. In the late nineteenth century there was a new interest in the practice of bodybuilding, and manuals appeared illustrated with photographs of 'Great Men's Bodies' of the past and present.[4] One pioneering advocate of physical culture who made extensive use of photography to promote his methods was the Frenchman Edmond Desbonnet. Visitors to his salons would be met by a display of photographs of the great athletes of the day, as well as before-and-after pictures demonstrating the effectiveness of his method. For men, Desbonnet promoted the well-muscled body of a Samson or a Mercury (277); for women the ideal was the roundness, serenity and grace of a Venus (278). Such nineteenth-century photographs of strongmen and proud athletes flexing their biceps were precursors to the flood of male muscle magazines which by the 1940s had released a torrent that has yet to abate.

A curious development in the late nineteenth century was a kind of proto-performance art in which semi-nude stage performers such as 'La Milo' or 'The Seldoms' would take up poses from famous sculptures, particularly those of **282** antiquity (275). The fad of the 'stage statue' or 'la statue humaine' was further popularized by mass distribution of photographic postcards, which, by freezing the pose, literally as well as figuratively, enhanced the illusion that what was being shown was real sculpture.

An amateur version of the new photographic idol was the beauty contest winner, of which the turn-of-the-century Miss Swim is a particularly graphic example (273). Here, for the camera of an anonymous photographer, she proudly displays her perfect hourglass figure, packaged in the latest seaside fashions.

Ideal male bodies in competition with each other were also commemorated by photographers like Bruce of Los Angeles (Bruce Bellas), one of the finest and most prolific of the breed of physique photographers who catered to homoerotic sensibilities (281).

For all their charm, the photographs of a Miss Swim or a Muscle Beach contest winner or a young hopeful having his body oiled by his mother in preparation for competition (280) appear relatively artless when compared with the typical studio genre. But, to be fair, their makers would never have claimed that they had anything more in mind than capturing a moment of personal triumph, and then disseminating the image as quickly and widely as possible. The motivating factor was not art, but business.

Yet their relative naivety makes these images more valuable as historical documents than the contrived studio images. Their appeal stems from the knowledge that we are looking back in time, at bodies which are literally no more, and, moreover, at bodies which are no longer seen as the temples of perfection they once were. Miss Swim's wasp-waist figure would have been viewed by her contemporaries as an ideal worthy of emulation; now we marvel at the extent to which – and how quickly – ideals of bodily perfection can change.

Professional celebrities of the twentieth century were to develop far more sophisticated notions of promotional photography, and would therefore make greater demands on it. They entrusted the making of their publicity photographs to experienced studio photographers who could be counted upon to take great pains to fabricate imagery which conformed to the glamorous construct already in people's minds. This required an equally polished 'performance' on the part of the subject. The fruit of such a collaboration can be seen in Madame d'Ora's shimmering vision of the cabaret star Josephine Baker (285). Many other Baker publicity photographs played on popular **283**

Maurice Beck
Girls Wrestling 1928
Gelatin silver print

(right) Madame d'Ora
Josephine Baker 1926
Gelatin silver print

prejudices equating black female nakedness with the 'primitive' and the 'natural'. Madame d'Ora took a different tack; her approach is typical of the soft-focus 'Ecole de Paris' nudes of the 1920s and 1930s, in which the art of the dance was often invoked as a legitimizing context for eroticism.

In the 1930s the German photographer and filmmaker Leni Riefenstahl brought a new sense of heroic glamour to the photography of athletes. Her work was rooted not in individual celebrity but in worship of the 'natural man', the being of sun and clean air, of 'sound mind in sound body', the superhuman being – Hitler's Aryan or Teutonic Man (287). Her Olympic idols took on the aspect of Greek Gods. Shot from worm's-eye and birds-eye perspectives, **284** beautifully modelled in light, seemingly defying gravity, the magnificent

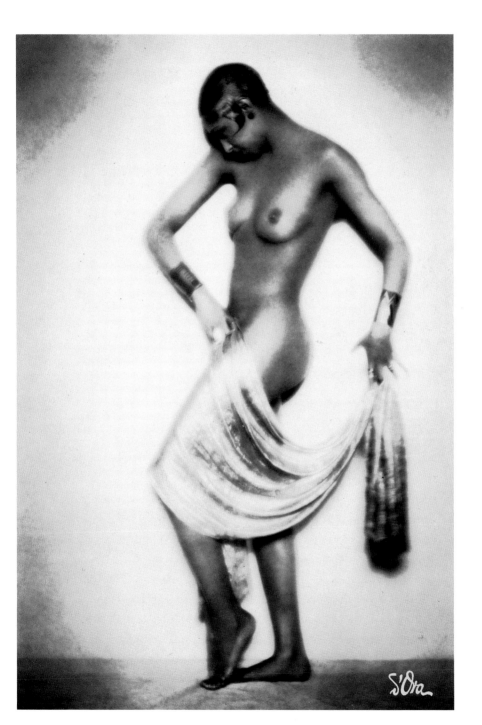

Robert Mapplethorpe
Derrick Cross 1985
Gelatin silver print

Leni Riefenstahl
Javelin Thrower, Olympic Games, Berlin 1936
Modern copy transparency

bodies must have convinced many impressionable minds of the supposed superiority of the German people.

By comparison with such pictorial ingenuity, the workmanlike promotional still of film star Raquel Welch made for the movie *One Million Years B.C.* strikes us as unadulterated kitsch (288). Yet who can honestly deny its appeal, an appeal which derives not just from its sexual lure, but from its recourse to an enduring myth – humankind in a primitive, more natural state, poised to do battle with the elements, and not yet softened by civilization. Here is a modern Eve, as Johnny Weissmuller had been a modern Adam for an earlier generation, not only with a beautifully conditioned body but also with a flair for the latest Stone Age fashion – the animal-skin bikini.   >>> **287**

Anonymous
Raquel Welch starring in *One Million Years B.C.* 1966
From original colour print

Burt Glinn
Chnstopher Reeve as Superman 1979
Colour transparency

Not all photographers who dwell on the theme of the ideal body are concerned with the promotion of icons and idols. Some prefer to deflate myths. Burt Glinn's backstage deconstruction pokes fun at one of America's most beloved heroes, Superman, here exposed as a weakling hardly fit to do battle with Charles Atlas (289). Canadian photographer Lynne Cohen confronts the beauty myth in *Spa* (*above*). Cohen is preoccupied with empty rooms of all kinds – offices, classrooms, lobbies, domestic interiors – spaces in which real bodies never intrude, having relinquished their rights in favour of two-dimensional visions of perfection. And with his *Electric Beauty*, the fashion photographer Horst P. Horst puts his glamourizing lens aside for a moment and gently mocks the phenomenal lengths to which many women will go in the pursuit of loveliness (*right*). □

290

(opposite) Lynne Cohen
Spa n.d.
Gelatin silver print

(above) Horst P. Horst
Electric Beauty 1938
Gelatin silver print

Max Yavno
Stockings by Sanderson c. 1940
Gelatin silver print

Herb Ritts
Vladimir, Hollywood 1990
Gelatin silver print

MIRROR

The mask is magic, character is not innate: a man's character is his demon, his tutelar spirit; received in a dream. His character is his destiny, which is to act out his dream.

NORMAN O. BROWN, *Love's Body*, 1966

When photographs first appeared a century and a half ago, people were astonished by their mirror-like fidelity. Early reports often referred to the 'mirror of nature' and 'the mirror with a memory.' Although today the ubiquity of photographic imagery has largely drained it of this awesome, magical aspect, some photographers have remained enthralled. So much so that they have turned their own bodies to the camera and found that, far from being confined to dumb reflections of surface realities, the photograph has offered a means with which to penetrate the deepest recesses of the self.

The earliest photographer to stage such an image was the Frenchman Hippolyte Bayard. He called the image, which featured himself as a half-naked corpse, 'portrait of a drowned man', thereby voicing his bitterness at not having been acknowledged as one of the inventors of photography. As early as 1840, therefore, there is a precursor to the theatrical stagings of the self so prevalent in photography of the late twentieth century.

Oscar Gustave Rejlander
Self-portrait c. 1857
Modern silver print

Another nineteenth-century antecedent exists in a self-portrait by the eminent Victorian photographer Oscar Gustave Rejlander, who was known for his highly moralistic genre scenes. Paradoxically, the photographer chooses on the one hand to expose himself to the camera, and on the other to shy away from it; the body is hidden beneath a sheet and the face shielded by the arm, almost as if Rejlander found the forthright gaze of the lens too much to bear (295).[1]

There are other significant late-nineteenth and early-twentieth-century precedents. Edvard Munch, for instance, made studies of his own naked or semi-naked body which convey the emotional and physical angst at the root of his art. The Polish avant-garde painter, writer and photographer Stanislaw Ignacy Witkiewicz focused closely on his own face, believing it to be a window through which the turbulence of the soul could be glimpsed (*right*).

Such unflinching explorations would encourage many late-twentieth-century photographers of the body. Whether it is the camera's tyranny over the body, as suggested by Rossella Bellusci's self-portrait (319), or the body living its life as a shadow, as Michel Szulc-Krzyzanowski proposes (308, 309), there is a fundamental urge to use photography as an instrument of self-discovery.

The Finnish-born photographer Arno Rafael Minkkinen seeks a spiritual rapprochement with the wide-open spaces of nature. Listening to voices deep within his psyche, he shapes his body in reply, often seemingly turning it inside out (310 *top and bottom*, 311). Some of Minkkinen's transformations look like totems, protective tribal emblems which take the form of real and imagined beings. One such totem adorns the prow of a boat; others are creatures which inhabit water; still another hovers motionless in the sky, literally suspended between heaven and earth, between spiritual aspirations and earthly constraints.

In his series *Immagini Scoperte* (*Discovered Images*) (320, 321), the Dutch photographer Jo Brunenberg makes an elegant blend of his photographs of the body with scientific drawings by Leonardo da Vinci. Here too there is a desire for transformation; we are reminded of the mythic figures of the constellations, and those of legend – a centaur, Icarus. The human body is ennobled, suggests Brunenberg, by the faculties of reason and imagination.[2]

We find an earthier vision in the imagery of German photographer Dieter Appelt (314-17). Both body and psyche are bared in strange sacrificial rites which hint at a primeval past. 'If the doors of perception were cleansed, every

Stanislaw Ignacy Witkiewicz
Self-portrait c. 1913
Gelatin silver print

thing would appear to man as it is, infinite,' wrote William Blake, and Appelt yearns for this clarity of vision. He is more than ready to leave behind the rough, brittle vessel of his body to achieve it; he waits impatiently in his 'Eye Tower', scanning the horizon for a sign, or he lies in his grave, willing death on.[3]

Of this urge on the part of artists to mirror the perilous state of their own being, the critic Max Kozloff has observed:

> . . . there runs through much of this work a shudder, as if at the thought that every breathing moment brought one closer to oblivion. In the last fifteen years a mental alarm of this general kind underlies fantasies of intolerable stress, of levitation and dying falls, of the body resting in suspended animation – a beautiful coma – and of afterlives or rebirths, organic or even earthy in their origin.[4]

In addition to photographers like Appelt, Kozloff was referring to various European and North American artists who, beginning in the 1960s and 1970s, took up the body itself as their medium, employing the camera – still and motion – as a primary means of documentation. >>> **297**

Lucas Samaras
Still Life 7.7.78 1978
Manipulated Polaroid print
Lucas Samaras
Self-portrait 6.14.90 1990
Manipulated Polaroid print

'Body artists' treated their own bodies as sculptural material – readily available and capable of great plasticity. Some believed that the body had to be used just like any other artists' material, subject to the same dispassionate tests and trials; others believed it had unique attributes which were worthy of attention, however banal. The simplest bodily functions – walking, breathing, picking one's nose – were invested with great solemnity. A spirit of Duchampian iconoclasm prevailed, tempered with irony and wit. But there was also a more masochistic vein, in which body artists cut, burnt, scarred, shot or otherwise abused their own bodies in order to bring neuroses and fears into the open.[5]

These 'bodyworks' could be highly exhibitionistic public events or wholly solitary rites performed in the artist's studio. What they had in common was that they were all ephemeral. Here the camera proved an indispensable tool; what were transitory, unique, unrepeatable moments were given permanent form in photographs. It is somewhat ironic, in view of the distaste with which many such artists viewed the traditional art object, that the photograph of the event, being all that remained of it, should inevitably take on this function. It is also true that without photography the 'body art' movement would not have received such widespread attention. After all, it is thanks only to the camera that Bruce Nauman's fountain continues to send its jet of water skyward twenty-five years after it was initially commemorated (304).

Although body art in general took no account of the aesthetics of fine art photography, some artists did treat photography as an integral aspect of their work rather than as a mere record-keeping device. In *I Box*, an early bodywork by Robert Morris, the artist housed an image of his naked body behind an I-shaped door, thus punning on visual and verbal ambiguities concerned with the essence of selfhood and the extent to which it could ever be truly revealed.

For one of the artists who has continued to work with her body, photography is 'less a tool than a partner'.[6] Since the early 1960s, Carolee Schneemann has made use of her naked body in solo performances, multi-media happenings and installations and has recorded her work extensively in photography and film (302-03). Celebrating the visceral, the animal, the sexual and the intuitive in works of sometimes Dionysian excess, she wields her body like a weapon, illuminating and subverting repressive cultural institutions and practices, particularly those which subjugate and degrade the female body and psyche.

Robert Morris
I Box 1962
Construction and photograph

Carolee Schneemann
Unexpectedly Research 1963–1991
16 colour prints

Schneemann also relies on photography in her researches – her 'visual archaeology'[7] as it has been called – into sacred or obscene representations of the female in matriarchal cultures.

In exposing their own bodies to the lens, all these artists and photographers lay themselves open to charges of narcissism and vanity. But intense scrutiny of the self in the hope of gaining some new insight about one's being, or about a generalized humanness, is not the same as self-absorption. Even a photographer as self 'centred' as Lucas Samaras, with three decades of exploration of the body

behind him, is constantly groping for further meaning and ever more profound

revelation (298, 299). Nor was self-love the motivation for Francesca Woodman's dreamlike self-reflections – on the contrary, they betrayed a fear that her body was merely an apparition or an object of fetishistic desire (322, 323).

Why should these idiosyncratic investigations interest us at all? Because we believe that somehow the artists are acting on our behalf, that we may learn something of ourselves from their struggles, their anguish, their hope. Arnulf Rainer's feverish twitchings (8) speak to, and for, all of us, and we are left to wonder if in the end the human spirit can ever find a comfortable accommodation with the flesh. □

Bruce Nauman
Myself as a Fountain 1967
Gelatin silver print

Henry Lewis
Untitled 1984
Gelatin silver print

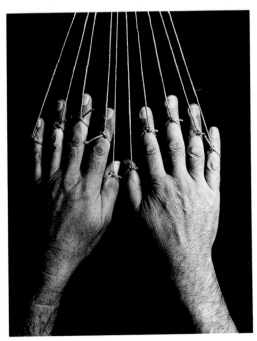

Henry Lewis
Untitled 1980
Gelatin silver print

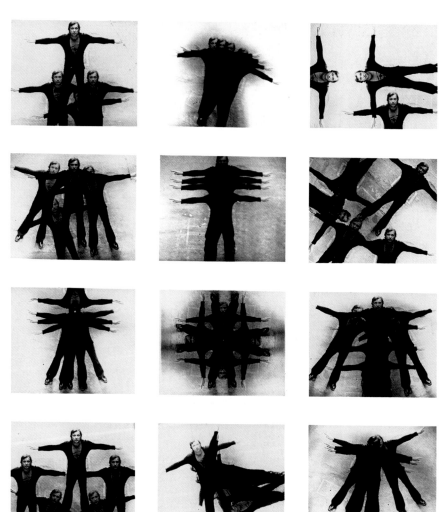

who

pulls

the

strings?

(opposite)
Andrzej Różycki
Icarus – A Photographic
Project of Picture Enlivening
1974
Gelatin silver prints

(left)
Suzy Lake
Choreographed Puppets
(Who Pulls the Strings) 1977
Gelatin silver prints

(overleaf above)
Michel Szulc-Krzyzanowski
Punta Boca, May 30 1984
Gelatin silver prints

(overleaf below)
Michel Szulc-Krzyzanowski
Baja California, Feb. 24 1980
Gelatin silver prints

307

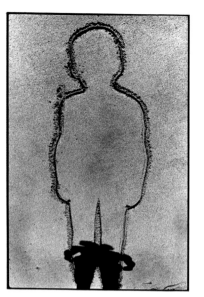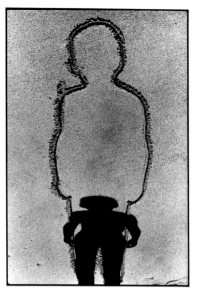

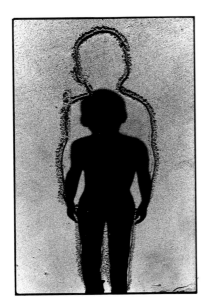

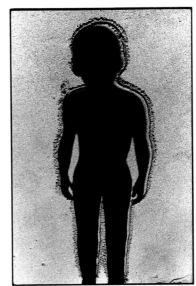

(opposite)
Arno Rafael Minkkinen
Kuopio, Finland 1987
Gelatin silver print

Arno Rafael Minkkinen
Fosters Pond 1992
Gelatin silver print

(above)
Arno Rafael Minkkinen
Naragansett, Rhode Island 1973
Gelatin silver print

Alain Fleischer
Le Couteau et la Cuillère (The Knife and the Spoon) 1985
Gelatin silver prints

(left) Dieter Appelt
Der Augenturm (The Eye Tower) 1977
Gelatin silver print

(above) Dieter Appelt
Erinnerungsspur (Trace of Memory) 1979
Gelatin silver print

315

Dieter Appelt
Der Augenturm (The Eye Tower) 1977
Gelatin silver print

Dieter Appelt
Erinnerungsspur (Trace of Memory) 1978
Gelatin silver print

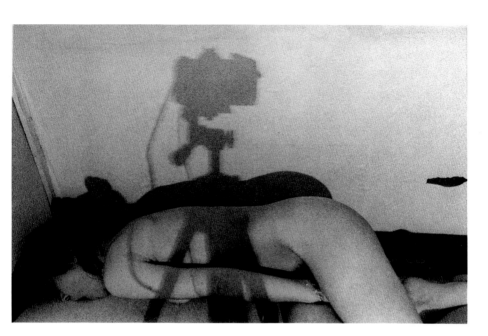

Rossella Bellusci
Autoportrait 1 (Self-portrait 1) 1980
Gelatin silver print

Roger Vulliez
Self-portrait 1984
Gelatin silver print

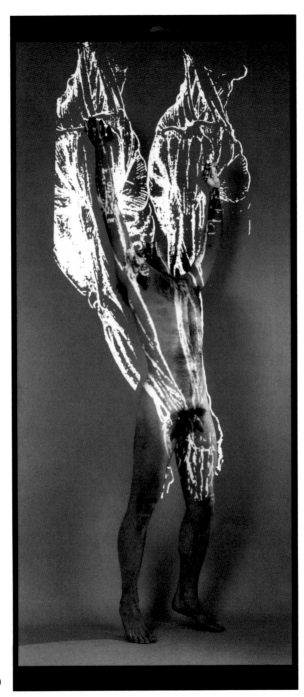

Jo Brunenberg
Studio dei muscoli del braccio (*Studies of the Muscles of the Arm*) (from the series *Immagini Scoperte/Discovered Images*) 1989 Selenium-toned silver print

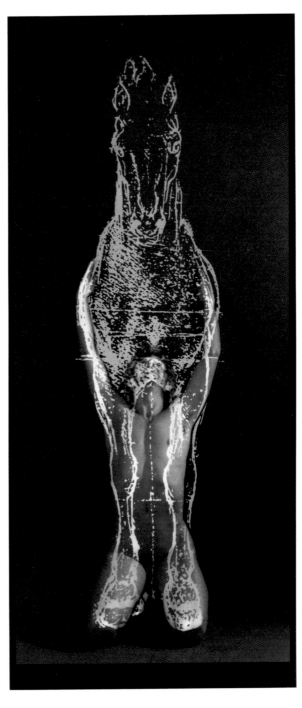

Jo Brunenberg
*Cavallo, visto di fronte
(Horse, Seen from the
Front)* (from the series
*Immagini Scoperte/
Discovered Images*) 1989
Selenium-toned
silver print

Francesca Woodman
On Being an Angel, Providence, Spring 1977
Gelatin silver print

Francesca Woodman
New York 1979-80
Gelatin silver print

POLITIC

The body is a highly contested site – its flesh is both the recipient and source of desire, lust and hatred. As a pawn of technology, it is sacred and sacrificial, bearing the politics of society and state. The body is our common bond, yet it separates us in its public display of identity, race and gender.

DAINA AUGAITIS, writing
on the work of HELEN CHADWICK

All photographs of the body are potentially 'political', inasmuch as they are used to sway our opinions or influence our actions. In this regard, an advertising image is as political as the most blatant propaganda. So is the supposedly autonomous art object, insofar as it represents fundamental attitudes and values. From a feminist viewpoint an Edward Weston study of a nude on a sand-dune makes questionable assumptions about the passivity of women, the youthful ideal of beauty, and about women's assumed harmony with nature (what critic Marina Warner has called the *nuda naturalis* motif in Western art[1]).

It is only because Weston's values were cultural bedrock – never questioned by most men and women – that his work was judged to be 'value-free'. It is in response to this that U.S. artist Kathy Grove performs her amusing deconstructions of famous photographs by Man Ray, André Kertész and others; by excising – she might say repossessing – the female form.

There are degrees to which the politics of an image are overt. Few photographers state their position as explicitly as Wladyslaw Bednarczuk in

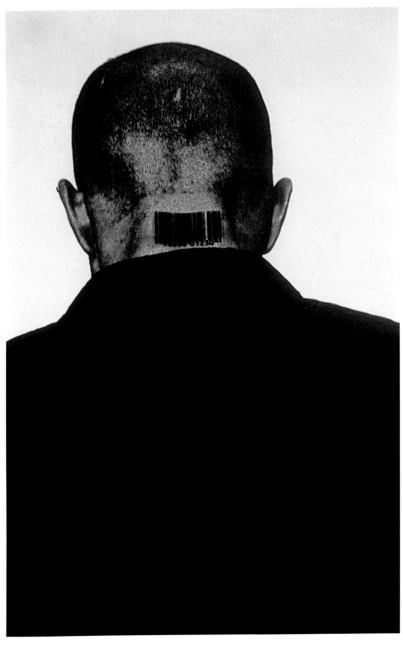

Jana Sterbak
Generic Man 1987
Duratran colour transparency

Wladyslaw Bednarczuk
Les Poings (The Fists) 1926
Photogravure

(opposite) Anonymous
Benito Mussolini *c.* 1935
Transparency from original print

The Fists, of 1926, an image which symbolizes left-wing solidarity (*above*). Likewise, the contemporary American photographer and model Matuschka is forthright in her call for a facing up to the uncomfortable issue of mastectomy. Her self-portrait, *Beauty out of Damage* (350), appeared on the cover of a 1993 *New York Times Magazine*, with the headline, 'You Can't Look Away Anymore'.

Ideological statements are sometimes more oblique. Take, for example, the anonymously made photograph of the Italian Fascist leader Benito Mussolini (*right*); a moment's consideration proves it to be something more than a casual snapshot, or 'reportage' of a famous individual on a skiing vacation; Mussolini poses as the virtual embodiment of the new Fascist masculine ideal – a tower of strength, self-confident, defying nature. Photographs of Mao swimming and **326** U. S. presidents jogging are variations on the same theme. >>>

Anonymous
Advertisement for Spellman shirts 1920
Gelatin silver print

Anonymous
The Man with the Diamond Dress 1920
Gelatin silver print

Claude Cahun
das Eva chanson c. 1930
Gelatin silver print

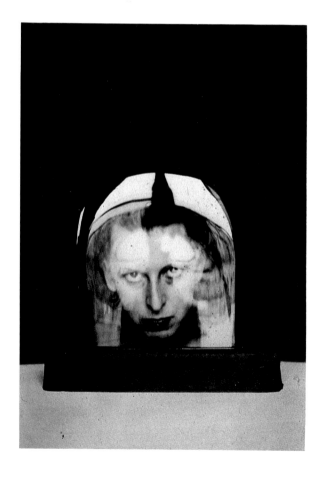

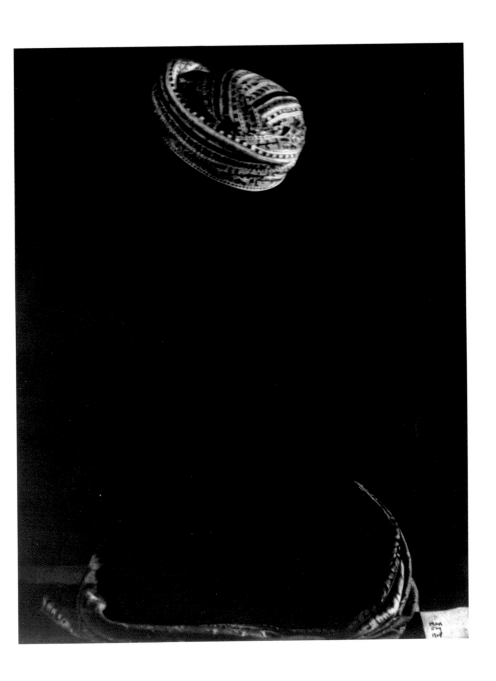

Kathy Grove
(The Other Series) After Man Ray 1990
Gelatin silver print

Nancy Burson
Androgyny 1982
Computer generated composite/gelatin silver print

Nancy Burson
Mankind 1983-84
Computer generated composite/gelatin silver print

Nancy Burson
Evolution II 1984
Computer generated composite/gelatin silver print

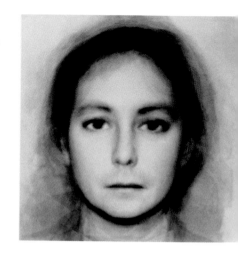

I have said that an image is political when it is *used* to sway our opinions because images are often appropriated for uses which were never intended by their makers. In the 1930s Nazi propagandists juxtaposed medical photographs of deformed and handicapped bodies with the distorted figures of Expressionist paintings to 'prove' the degeneracy of the artists and thereby justify censorship. In our own time, 'Pro Life' demonstrators hold up a medical photograph of a foetus in the womb to attack what they see as the inhuman practice of abortion, while a clothing manufacturer appropriates an image of a man dying of AIDS for an advertisement. Where politics are concerned, context is all.

Certain contemporary photographers and artists have taken on the task of examining, exposing and subverting these political, economic and technological ideologies, while others have focused on pathologies which lie closer to the surface of the body politic – on prejudice, exploitation and wilful ignorance.

The conceptual and pictorial strategies that have been adopted are diverse, but it may be helpful to think in terms of three main approaches. First, there is so-called straight photography, meaning that the photographer documents a given situation (350); then there are theatrical or staged works, in which an actor (sometimes the photographer) plays a stereotypical role in order to have it critically examined (344); third, there are (literally) images which disassemble found imagery and reassemble its parts (338); lastly, there are synthetic works, constructed from images and text (337).

332

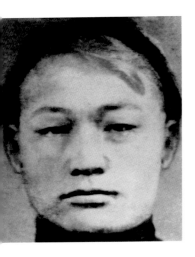

The dangers implicit in the worship of technology and a blind faith in scientific progress are recurrent themes. Artist Jana Sterbak's victim suffers the ignominy of having a bar code stamped onto his neck, a warning to us all that in a consumerist society the body is nothing more than another commercial product to be monitored and controlled (325).

Lynne Cohen's *Laboratory* sounds a similar note of unease over our faith in technology (353). This bizarre site, with its mise-en-scène which strives to project an image of cool, scientific investigation, strikes us more as a factory, in which bodies are just pieces of hardware to be tuned up for enhanced performance.

Photographer Mike Mandel is more ambivalent. As what he calls 'a born-again Gilbreth' (referring to the pioneers of time-and-motion analysis), he believes that many of the dehumanizing tasks bodies have had to perform could well be taken over by machines.[2] But relinquishing control is not without risk; Mandel's frenetic *Robot* threatens to push the real body aside (352).

Nancy Burson, on the other hand, embraces advanced technology, making it the medium of her art (*above*). Using complex computer programmes devised in collaboration with Richard Carling and David Cramlich, she creates composite 'generic' portraits of human beings – an androgyne (consisting of six men and six women); 'Mankind' (a being made up of individuals of three races, each weighted according to a proportion of the population) and what we might call a 'humanimal' (a composite of man and chimpanzee). Too often, Burson suggests, **333** human beings are instructed in their *differences* – of gender, sexual orientation, race, even their supposed distances from their animal ancestors – rather than being reminded of the body as a common bond.

A similar sentiment is expressed in Michelle Bradford's *Pierced Hermaphrodite* (341). This hypothetical being compounded of fragmentary photographs of the bodies of four men and women – 'neither sex, yet both' – forces the viewer to rethink notions of difference and separation, or, in the photographer's words, 'all the possible ways of joining and of gaining sexual intimacy'.[3]

In Richard Hamilton's *Fashion-plate*, photographs of models' faces taken from magazines such as *Vogue* and *Harper's Bazaar* have been cut into pieces and collaged onto a 'set' which suggests a fashion photographer's studio (338). Paint, pastels and – mimicking the beautification of the face itself – cosmetics have been applied to the surface of the work. In this way, Hamilton deconstructs the glamour myth perpetuated by fashion journals.

Robert Walker's collage *Nice n' Easy* juxtaposes 1970s advertising imagery with a poster from China's cultural revolution, so bringing into sharp relief the propagandistic strategies of two opposing ideologies (339). The seductive ploys of Western consumerism are pitted against the strident claims of Chinese Communism, with unexpected results – the stereotypically 'passive' oriental woman stares fiercely into the future, while her pampered occidental counterpart looks demurely downward, her face veiled by luxuriant hair.

Robert Heinecken also works with found imagery to question issues of sexuality and exploitative media representation (340). He begins with photographs of naked female bodies taken from erotic magazines; fragments of the photographs – faces, breasts, torsos and thighs – are then ingeniously recombined as if they were pieces of a puzzle, and subtly 'retouched' in a way which heightens the erotic element while simultaneously engendering a feeling of intense claustrophobia.

If there is common ground for feminist photographers and artists, it is that there is no pre-existing, absolute sexuality, no given masculinity or femininity, only cultural constructs, and that in a patriarchal system these constructs must inevitably operate to the disadvantage of women. In a culture which sets great store by visual communication, the photographic image is a potent weapon in **334** maintaining the status quo and must therefore be subjected to scrutiny and, ultimately, to subversion of its repressive functions. Aesthetics, too, are political. Hugely influential in deconstructing the politics of representation are the American artists Barbara Kruger and Cindy Sherman. Kruger combines word and image to produce a dramatic and subversive art in the style of the poster (337). Sherman uses her own body as a template from which to examine a host of issues relating to the mass media's representations of femininity. In her famous 1977-1980 series of *Film Stills* she 'plays' stereotypical female roles in stagings from fictive B-movies (349). Her repertoire of bored housewife, pampered mistress, jilted lover, teenage hitchhiker and so on serve to undermine and condemn such reactionary, neo-romantic conceptions of the modern women. Likewise, her portrayals of men in 'great paintings' mock the invisibility of women in both art and history (344).

Although contemporary British artist Helen Chadwick believes that attention must be paid to the issue of female identity in order to redress the historical imbalance, her ultimate goal is insight into the universal human condition. Identity, sexuality, gender, animality and the like are too complex to be approached directly; 'seeing' is an oblique process, requiring the manipulation of signs and symbols. Is the body a specimen, a machine, a vessel, an archetype, heat, light, beast – meat (342)? Can it ever know itself? Of Chadwick's piece *Eroticism* (343) the question might be asked: How can *two* bodies, *two* minds, ever achieve mutual comprehension? The artist herself writes:

> . . . two brains lie enraptured, exposed to our gaze, yet we witness the field of their activity, the turbulence of the fabric they lie on. Is this a single brain mirrored, or two individualities? An open locket or a bed? Is eroticism a reciprocal exchange between two or a blind narcissistic projection of oneself towards an unseeable other?[4]

Like other artists of her generation, Chadwick suggests that the path to an understanding of the larger social body – the body politic – lies in a fuller knowledge of one's own flesh. □

Annie Sprinkle
Anatomy of a Pinup Photo 1991 (photograph by Zorro, 1981)
Postcard

ANATOMY OF A PIN UP Photo: Mandatory Fake beauty mark.
• False Eyelashes
• Extra Blush
• eyebrows penciled in
• Hair dyed to cover some gray.
• Red lipstick
• Hair put into HOT Rollers for curling but it creats dryness + Split ends.
• Breasts are real but sag. Bra lifts breasts.
• Pucker gives suggestion of a blow job
• Bra is a size too small to make breasts look bigger.
• Lungs restricted. I cannot brethe.
• Body make-up.
• Corset hides a very big belly.
• Hemeroids don't show, thank goodness.
• CORSET MAKES my WAIST 4½" smaller, but I can't brethe.
• I need assistance to hook all these garters, and to lace back of corset.
• I never wear gloves except in pin-up photos.
• Extra tall stockings make my legs look longer.
• Black stockings make legs look thinner.
• Gloves cover tattoos for a more All American girl effect Barrowed from Antionette.
• Boots take 19 minutes to lace up. I need assistance to lace them because I can't bend over in the corset.
• I can't walk and can barely hobble.
• A plexiglass square keeps the white seamless paper from smudging.
• These heels are excruciatingly high.
• Boots are 1½ sizes too small. Barrowed and worn only for this shoot.
• My feet are killing me.
(In spite of it all, Im sexually excited AND feeling great.)

336

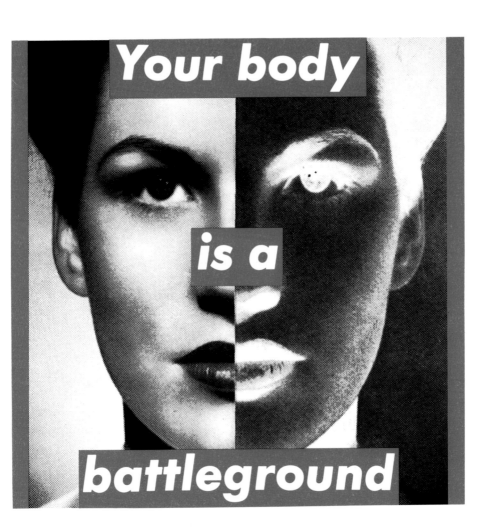

Barbara Kruger
Untitled 1989
Photosilkscreen/vinyl

Richard Hamilton
Fashion-plate 1969-70
Photo-offset lithograph, collage, screenprint, pochoir and retouching with cosmetics

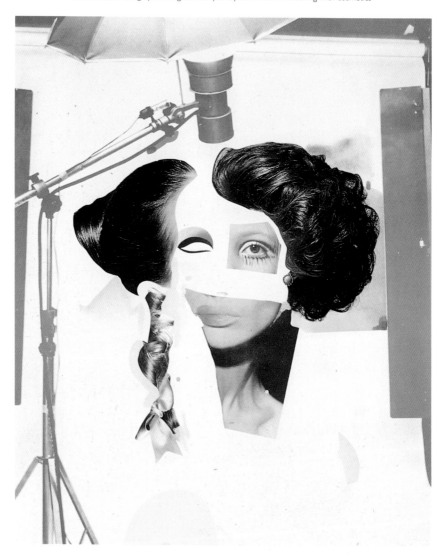

Robert Walker
Nice 'n Easy 1976
3M Color-in-Color copier prints/montage

Robert Heinecken
Clichy Vary/Fetishism 1974
Gelatin silver print, coloured with pastel and chalk

Michelle Bradford
Pierced Hermaphrodite 1993
Photographic montage

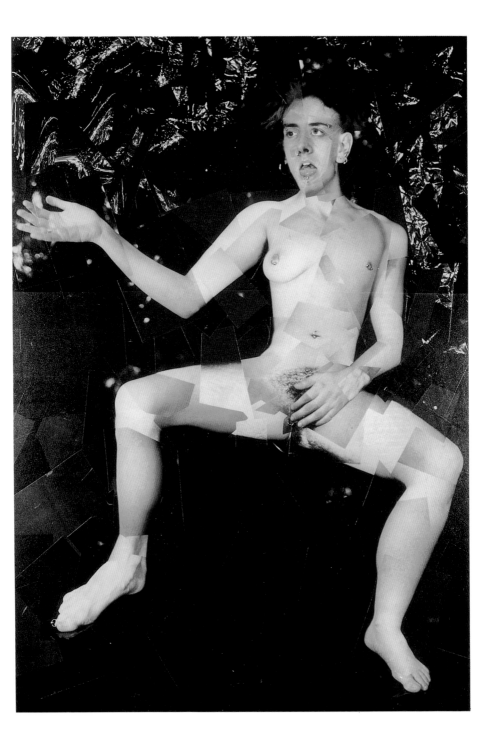

Helen Chadwick
Enfleshings II 1989
Cibachrome transparency, glass, steel, electric apparatus

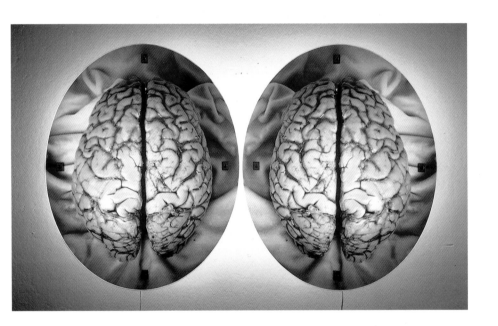

Helen Chadwick
Eroticism 1990
Cibachrome transparencies, glass, aluminium, electric apparatus

Carolee Schneemann
Forbidden Actions - Museums 1979
Photosilkscreen

Cindy Sherman
Untitled, #224 1990
Colour photograph

345

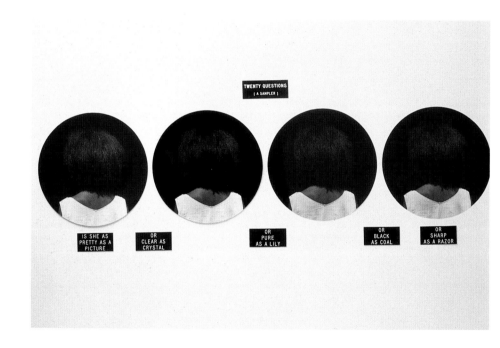

Lorna Simpson
Twenty Questions (A Sampler) 1986
4 gelatin silver prints, 6 engraved plastic plaques

Lorna Simpson
Same 1991
16 colour Polaroid prints, 11 engraved plastic plaques

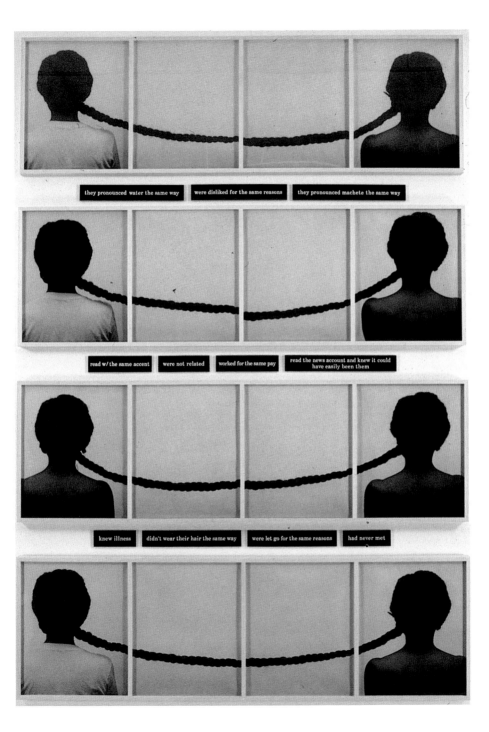

Laurie Simmons
Lying Gun 1990
Gelatin silver print

Cindy Sherman
Untitled Film Still, #39 1977
Gelatin silver print

Matuschka
Beauty out of Damage 1993
Gelatin silver print from colour original

Janusz Maria Brzeski
Lesbos II 1930
Photocollage   **351**

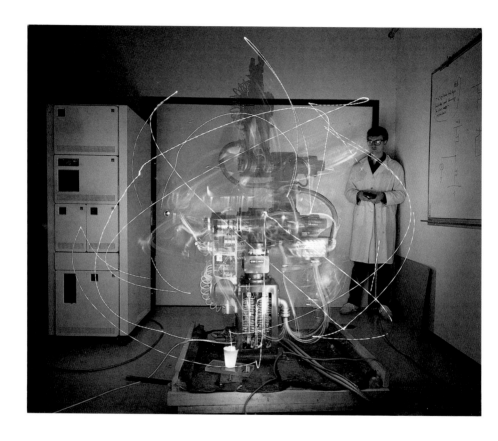

Mike Mandel
Robot 1984
Colour transparency

Lynne Cohen
Laboratory n.d.
Gelatin silver print

METAMORPHOSIS

Day and night I try, in my studio with its six two-thousand watt suns,
balancing between the extremes of the impossible, to shake loose the
real from the unreal, to give visions body, to penetrate into unknown
transparencies.

ERWIN BLUMENFELD
My Hundred Best Photos, 1979

There is a story about Picasso, apocryphal perhaps, in which the artist is showing a client a portrait he has painted of the man's wife. The husband doesn't like the portrait. 'My wife doesn't look like that,' he complains. The painter asks what she does look like, whereupon the man pulls out a snapshot from his wallet. 'Like this,' he says. 'How extraordinary,' replies Picasso, 'I had no idea she was so small!'

The story should remind us that all photographs, however 'real' they appear, involve radical transformations, dramatically so where the scale, the cropping of the frame, and the compression of space into two dimensions are concerned. Ironically, it would probably be a life-size photographic nude which would shock us most if encountered on a gallery wall. We are used to five- or six-inch bodies, with all the particularities of the originals – birthmarks, moles, cuts, scratches, peeling skin – reduced to a finely grained, homogeneous texture. So that even the so-called naturalistic nude is a smooth deception.

The earlier sections dealing with figure, fragment and flesh have shown how the body can be of aesthetic interest in and of itself. It may be stretched to colossal proportions, or fragmented, or seen from a disorienting angle, but it remains recognizably the human body. There is, however, another tendency, one in which the body is seen to undergo more fundamental change, as if it longs to

Bill Brandt
Baie des Anges 1959
Gelatin silver print

break free of its own material constraints, or those imposed upon it by the laws of nature. In such photographs the flesh can defy gravity, anatomy, biology, time and reason. It dissolves into or fuses with nature, merges with objects or metamorphoses into alien human or animal forms.

Among the most haunting and enigmatic of such transformations are the fragmentary forms created by the great British photographer Bill Brandt (355). Brandt had a long involvement with the nude before he was impelled to dismember the body, strewing its segments along the beaches of England and France. There they sit, absolutely immobile, like ancient monuments of obscure purpose, possibly beacons or sentinels weathering wind and wave. Some we recognize after a momentary disorientation as parts of the human body – an ear, intertwined fingers, soles of feet, crossed knees, while others, amorphous lumps or mounds of some strange composite of flesh and stone, remain perplexing, indecipherable.

What inspired Brandt to produce these wholly original transformations? Perhaps he felt that his earlier, more or less full-figure, nudes were too specific in regard to identity, time and place. They had not succeeded, as the fragments would, in conveying a sense of the universal human condition, that which is measured in eons, rather than in the lifespan of a mere individual.

André Kertész's playful, amusing series of nude distortions of 1933 are worlds apart from Brandt's sombre reflections (361, 362). Kertész used a distorting mirror of the kind encountered in a fun-house to stretch, compress and 'clone' female bodies. Contours are wildly exaggerated. Limbs dissolve into spidery wisps; breasts and buttocks are inflated like balloons. Heads sprout feet, or from each other, like amoebas. Brandt's vision was about permanence and stone; Kertész's women seem to have been heated to their melting point, then remoulded as fantastic shapes.

Kertész may not have been aware that there were precedents of a sort in late-nineteenth-century amateur photography, where we find bodies provided with two heads or three feet, or severed heads smiling for their portraits, all created by the clever use of mirrors and darkroom trickery. But Kertész was a serious artist, well aware of the radical transformations the body had undergone or was undergoing at the hands of Cubists, Futurists and Surrealists. A number of Salvador Dali's paintings of the late twenties and early thirties show striking similarities with the Kertész distortions. One of them, *Birth of Liquid Desires* (1932), might well have provided Kertész with a title for his series. The amorphous, ballooning bodies of Picasso's *Bather* series are also spiritual cousins, and may even have proved something of an inspiration. But the Kertész distortions are never grotesque or cruel. They do not mock or assault the female anatomy, but rather delight in remodelling it.

Mirror distortions were fundamental to the visionary stagecraft of the German-born photographer Erwin Blumenfeld, best known today as a highly influential fashion photographer of the postwar period. For Blumenfeld, who freely admitted to an obsession with the female body, the studio transaction between model and camera was often only the starting point on the road to the final image; to escape banality, 'magical' intervention was called for. The alchemy was performed in the darkroom through a variety of optical and chemical manipulations. Here the body could be transformed from a creature of flesh and blood into an apparition, perhaps an archaic fertility goddess like the *Venus of Willendorf* (379).

Quite obviously, the body can be subjected to an infinite number of photographic transformations and reconfigurations. The game may be played as one of signs and symbols, of specific equivalences between the properties, parts or functions of the body and those of some other being or thing, as, for example, in Steef Zoetmuller's sensuous blending of animate and inanimate 'vessels' (382) and Man Ray's literal elevation of the female body to high art (383). Or the game may be played as one of more open-ended speculation, as in Ray K. Metzker's elegant, kaleidoscopic, high-contrast composites, where some scrutiny is required in order to locate the human form (367). This stimulation of the imagination is precisely what is intended. 'I am not an objective reporter,' Metzker reminds us, 'I prefer to go further, to the unstated things of our existence. What I can't understand and grasp seems to lead me.'[1]

This is a statement of purpose with which each of the photographers represented here would probably agree – Barbara Crane, for example, who demonstrates that the wholeness of the body and the soft pliancy of the flesh can be evoked with minimal means in a most stylish manner (380, 381); or Florence Chevallier, who searches for the essence of the body not in stillness and clearly delineated form, but in the traces of its ceaseless mobility (363, 364).   **357**

Doug Prince achieves his unique transformations through transference. Prince asked himself whether the living body might not also be made 'a part of the process as well as the subject matter'[2] if it were put directly in contact with light-sensitive materials, bypassing the camera. The results were far from the mirror-like images one might have expected from a direct transcription (370, 371). They evoke something primeval, or fossilized, and conjure up images of vast landscapes seen from a great height.

Holly Wright's bodies are very real – and wholly illusory. The muscled torsos, the straining necks, the buttocks pressed together – all are figments of the imagination, or rather a joint imagination, ours as well as Wright's (368, 369, 376, 377). Contrary to appearances, these are photographs only of their maker's hands and fingers. But they are more than an amusing variation on the theme of figure and fragment; once aware of the deception we are persuaded to look at this commonplace object anew, like Roquentin in Sartre's *Nausea*: 'I see my hand spread out on the table. It lives – it is me . . . It is lying on its back. It shows me its fat belly. It looks like an animal upside down.'[3]

Ernestine Ruben refuses to accept human anatomy as a given. Her bodies are assembled according to the dictates of her imagination; parts of one body detach and recombine with those of another (378). 'The words required here are fused words, words of the senses,' notes critic Derek Bennett, 'Run the hand of your eye over the shoulder of stone. Run the hand of your eye down the curved back of the ground. Now seek to run the hand of your eye between the stone and the shoulder.'[4] It is not the individual identity of the body, the envelope of a unique 'self' that interests Ruben, but the body 'spoken' as a universal tongue. □

Ralph Gibson
New York City 1988
Gelatin silver print

André Kertész
Distortion No. 86 c. 1933
Gelatin silver print

Erwin Blumenfeld
Untitled 1949
Solarized gelatin silver print

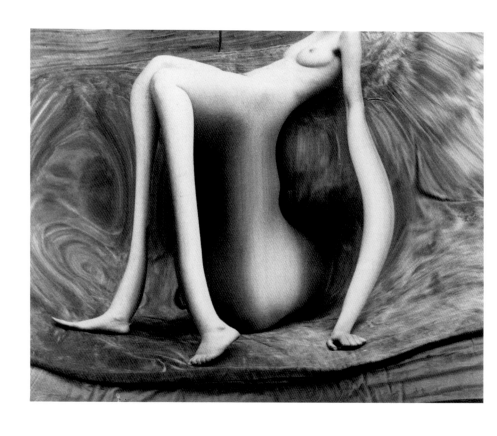

André Kertész
Distortion No. 141 c. 1933
Gelatin silver print

Florence Chevallier
Nude, Naples 1986
Gelatin silver print

Florence Chevallier
Nude Self-portrait 1985
Gelatin silver print

Wilhelm Helg
Magnetic Man Ray 1993
Manipulated photocopy print

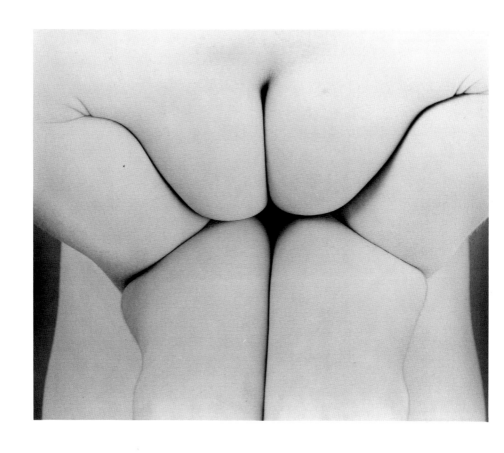

Pierre Radisic
Sonja 1987
Gelatin silver print

Ray K. Metzker
Nude Composite 1966-90
Gelatin silver print

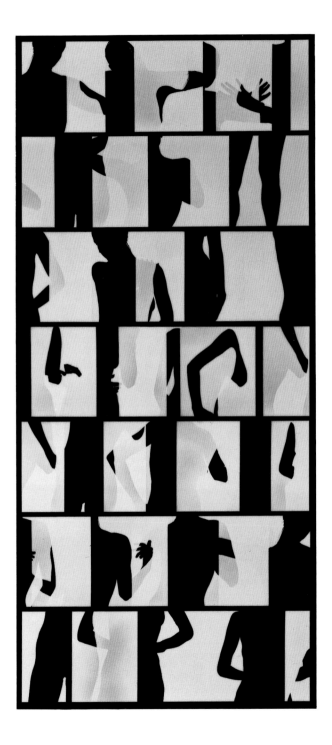

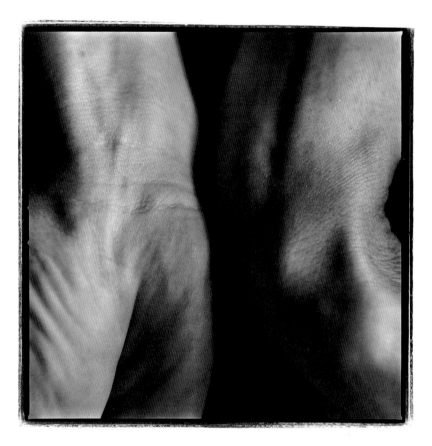

(above and opposite)
Holly Wright
Untitled, from the series *Vanity* 1985-88
Gelatin silver print

(overleaf)
Doug Prince
Shoulder, Imprint No. 7 1993
Gelatin silver print

369

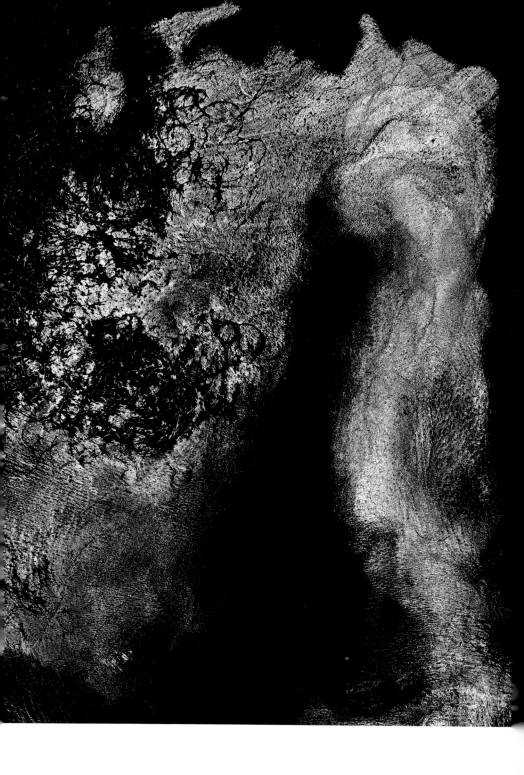

Emmet Gowin
Edith 1986
Toned silver print

Harry Callahan
Eleanor, Aix-en-Provence c. 1958
Gelatin silver print

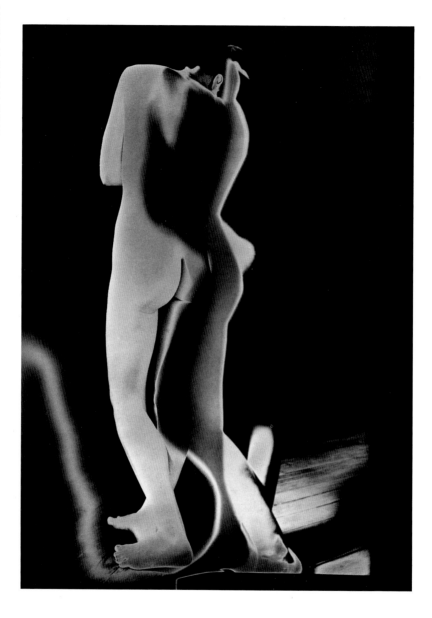

Jacqueline Feldine
Relaxing 1986
Solarized gelatin silver print

Jacqueline Feldine
The Wave 1988
Solarized gelatin silver print

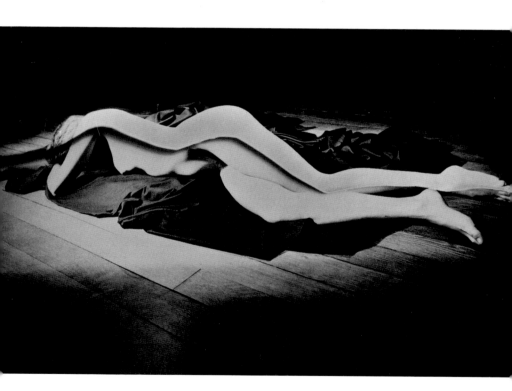

Holly Wright
Untitled, from the series *Vanity* 1985-88
Gelatin silver print

Holly Wright
Untitled, from the series *Vanity* 1985-88
Gelatin silver print

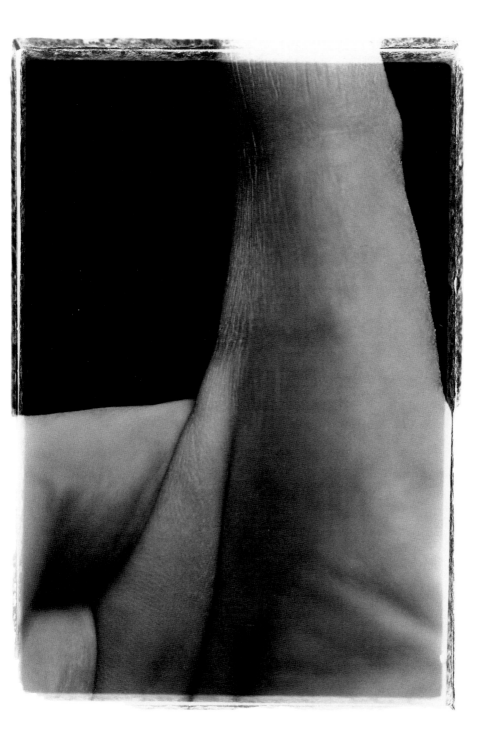

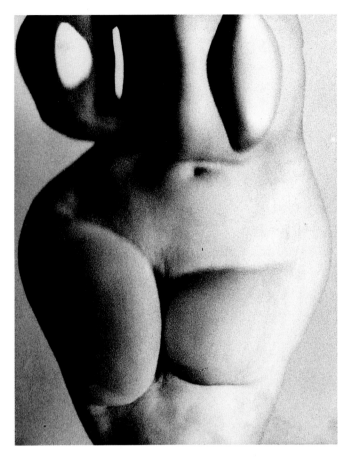

Erwin Blumenfeld
Untitled c. 1948-49
Gelatin silver print

Ernestine Ruben
Teenage Arms 1981
Gelatin silver print

379

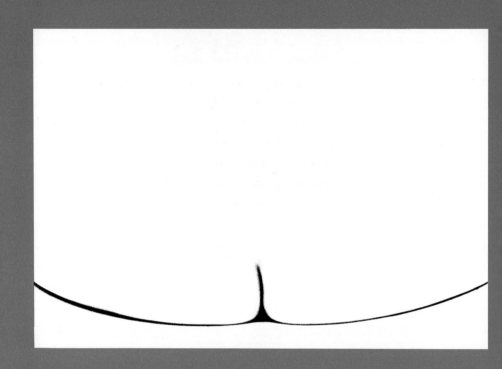

Barbara Crane
Human Form 1965
Gelatin silver print

Barbara Crane
Human Form 1965
Gelatin silver print

Man Ray
Untitled 1930
Gelatin silver print

Steef Zoetmulder
Nude with Vase c. 1948
Gelatin silver print

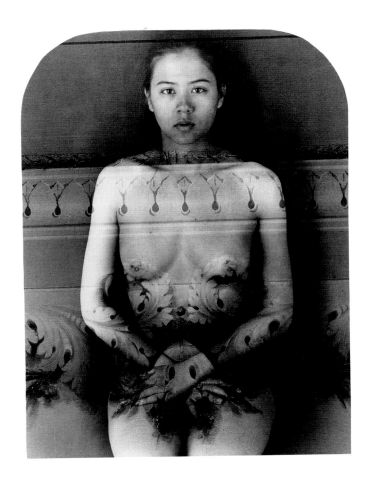

George Woodman
Vivienne in Calci 1992
Gelatin silver print

Tono Stano
Sense 1992
Gelatin silver print

MIND

*Only a puritan would disagree, seeing in the body only gross matter
and a despicable magma of viscera, rather than a mysterious theater
which provides a stage for all exchange – whether of matter, mind,
or the sense – between inner and outer worlds.*

MICHEL LEIRIS

Must the body *exist* to be photographed? By no
means, say the photographers in this section,
some of whom invent bodies at will, coaxing them
out of the chemistry and optics of the medium,
fabricating them from parts of dolls, or piecing them
together from reproductions scavenged from magazines
and postcards. Others appropriate bodies from anatomical drawings and models, famous paintings and sculptures,
and even historical photographs. Still others begin their work
with a *real* body but transform it in various ways – painting on
it prior to photographing it, for example, or reworking the image
in the film negative or on the surface of the print itself.

Fantasies, obsessions and dreams find a place in these fabrications. Bodies can
be given strange and wonderful attributes, or fashioned into mythic beings such
as mermaids and Amazons, or made weightless, headless, transparent. Body
fragments may be induced to dance on a stage, or navigate a ship through a
storm. The photographer may refuse to bow to the laws of man or nature – to
gravity, perspective, time, propriety and common sense.

There is enormous variation in the degree of sophistication in these
hallucinatory images. At one end of the spectrum are charming – if crude –
nineteenth-century transformations of bodies accomplished by means of trick

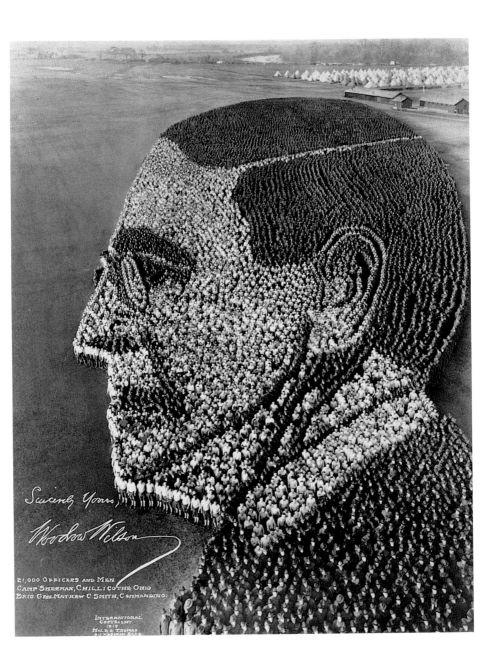

Mole & Thomas
21,000 Officers and Men, Camp Sherman, Chillicothe, Ohio. Brig. Gen. Mathew C. Smith Commanding 1918
Gelatin silver print

Guerin
Untitled c. 1890
Gelatin silver print

photography or the retoucher's brush, such as the sea creatures concocted by the commercial studio of Guerin as publicity material for actresses (*above* and *right*). At the other are complex, articulate works of art which address profound issues relating to corporeality.

Naive photography, however, can still be imaginative, as the firm of Mole & Thomas proves with its monumental portrait of the American president Woodrow Wilson (387). Miraculously, this has been accomplished without the presence of the great man himself; instead, the 21,000 military men of Camp Sherman 'embody' their commander-in-chief in a spectacular tribute not only to the man but to the strength of the 'body politic'.

The advent of avant-garde art in the early twentieth century had a liberating effect on many photographers. From the 1920s to the 1940s, Surrealism appealed enormously to many Europeans who had previously felt that the

verisimilitude of photography had ruled out metaphysical speculation. The

Guerin
Untitled c. 1890
Gelatin silver print

German photographer Herbert List, for example, seems to have been influenced by De Chirico's musings (395). At the same time, certain painters and designers were equally impressed by photography's unique ability to administer psychic shock. Newly minted techniques such as solarization, negative printing, multiple exposure and montage could effect dreamlike transformations that were irresistible to both camps, and the cutting-up of found imagery and its rearrangement on the page was recognized as a new and potent metaphor for the turbulence and fragmentation of the machine age. Nothing could be more shocking than a fragmented human body, especially when the fragments were recombined with animals, objects and machines.

The Czech artist Karel Teige was a leading exponent of the new genre, trapping his dehumanized figures in webs of steel (414). In Poland, Aleksander Krzywoblocki and Kazimierz Podsadecki championed the Surrealist approach. Krzywoblocki, who was both an architect and a photographer, was fascinated by **389** the relationship of the body to built structures (415). Podsadecki, a painter, designer and something of an experimental filmmaker, used montage and collage to warn against excessive worship of machines, while stressing the body's own wondrous workings. His *Venus B* (404) is a witty melange of symbols musing on the myriad ways in which we seek to shed light on a subject otherwise shrouded in darkness: through works of art, anatomical investigation and the written word.

No Surrealist vision is more disturbing than the nightmare shared with us by the sex-obsessed German photographer Hans Bellmer (400). Using an articulated plaster doll which could be assembled in any number of ways, Bellmer gave voice to his deepest erotic obsessions and fears. 'I want to reveal scandalously the interior which will always remain hidden and sensed,' he has said, 'I agree with Georges Batailles that eroticism relates to a knowledge of evil and the inevitability of death, it is not simply an expression of joyful passion.'[1]

The Surrealist vision of the body as it manifested itself in photo-collage and montage was a decidedly European one, and where we find American examples these roots are evident. Both Max Ernst and Salvador Dali are obvious influences in the work of the Romanian-born American artist Andre Racz (410). Racz practised the Surrealist credo of automatism, typically combining balloon-shaped bodies with shells and other organic forms, and adding sweeping lines which animated the image and suggested trajectories of these lighter-than-air beings through space.

The Japanese photographer Minayoshi Takada was deeply influenced both by Surrealism and by experimental photography of the interwar period. Shortly after the Second World War he began work on a series of highly innovative images of the female body using double exposure and other manipulative darkroom techniques to create visions in which the landscape seems to flow in and through the female body (417). The contemporary body-painters Holger Trülzsch and Vera Lehndorff also admit to the lure of Surrealism, to the extent that it celebrates the imagination, though they reject Surrealism's worship of the unconscious and its obsession with the transformation of the female body into a fetishized object. For Lehndorff and Trülzsch, the surfaces of the *real* world are to be explored with minute attention to detail in order to reveal 'a secret world, a new aspect.'[2] They accomplish this collaboratively by painting directly on to

Lehndorff's body and photographing the results. The painting has the effect of fusing the body with the environment, which may be either natural or man-made: if the latter, the body becomes a part of peeling walls, cracked paint, wires, bolts, hinges and rusting pipes – as Lehndorff puts it, 'a place of decay . . . related to our culture' (406).[3] Photography enhances the fusion; transcribed as a two-dimensional image on the surface of the paper, the painted body is found to be *no less real* than the environment in which it is situated.

The French artist Annette Messager, who has used photographs ingeniously and provocatively for twenty years, explains how they serve her imagination:

> I stick eyes back on
> I unstick ears
> I cut off fingers
> I tear off a breast
> this is my law of exchanges
> I carve up
> I pull to pieces . . .
> . . . I give birth only to chimera[4]

One of Messager's many techniques is to draw and paint on the surface of the body itself, covering hands, buttocks, knees and feet with folkartish, quasi-religious depictions of imaginary creatures and scenes, 'something half-way between a fairy-tale and a nightmare' (408).[5] By inscribing these fantasies on so 'lowly' a part of the body as the foot she reminds us that no aspect of the human body is less miraculous than the images conjured up by the mind. She calls her painted body parts 'my trophies'.

Messager's countryman Rémy Fenzy has a similar interest in the fusion of painting, photography and the body. Inspired by a passage in Proust's *Swann's Way* in which the protagonist is moved by the striking resemblance of Odette to a figure on a fresco in the Sistine Chapel, Fenzy searches for such similarities between people he meets and the subjects of famous paintings, preferably portraits.[6] Using a black-and-white reproduction of the painted figure and a portrait he takes of the actual individual, he makes a composite in his darkroom by superimposing the two negatives, as, for example, in his blend of a young man with Egon Schiele's *Nude in Red Loincloth, 1914* (419). Fenzy's choice of painter here is revealing – he has voiced admiration for the work of Arnulf

Rainer (8) and Schiele's uncompromising treatment of the body is not unlike that of the contemporary German photographer.

Painting has proved to be a rich source of inspiration for many photographers. It is likely that the contemporary Czech photographer Pavel Baňka was influenced by Henry Fuseli's *Nightmares*, though he clearly also owes a debt to his eminent predecessor František Drtikol (413). Lucas Cranach was an inspiration for the *Adam and Eve* which Scottish artist Ron O'Donnell fabricated in his studio and then photographed (403). American artist Holly Roberts, on the other hand, uses a photographic image of a body both as a stimulus and as an actual base for her painting. She lays the image down on canvas and then layers paint onto it, projecting her sense of that body's full potential (402).

British conceptual artist John Stezaker plunders visual imagery of the body from magazines and postcards to make witty photo-collages which intentionally disrupt the signals that the original images were meant to transmit. In a series begun in 1990, Stezaker worked with images from a Scandinavian nudist magazine, cutting out a figure and then turning the page over to see what the correspondence was with the body on the other side (407). If the empty shape was intriguing, he filled it with a reproduction of an eighteenth-century painting; in the collage shown here, the space has been filled by an image of a domestic interior. In each work, therefore, there are two figures seen simultaneously: one on the outside (the black-and-white nude) and one on the inside (the filled-in outline).

Louis Aragon wrote: 'For each man there awaits. . . a particular image capable of annihilating the entire universe.'[7] For Joel-Peter Witkin that image was an 1850s nude by the pioneering French photographer and painter Charles Nègre. Witkin was inspired to restage – in fact, to relive – this image for three reasons. The first was the work itself, which struck him as one of uncommon sensuality and beauty; the second was a chance encounter with a woman who desperately wished to pose for him and who bore a striking resemblance to the model in the nineteenth-century photograph; and the third was Witkin's discovery of a book on foot fetishism (418).[8]

By putting himself in the role of Nègre, and his model in the role of his predecessor's model, Witkin was hoping to experience something of the sensual current which he believes must have flowed between the original pair. The magical extensions he placed on his model's feet were in essence a projection of his own sexual yearnings for this beautiful woman, yearnings which he forcibly sublimated into his art. 'We consummated our union aesthetically', explains Witkin, 'not through the act of sex.'[9] Thus, *Nègre, Fetishist* is both an homage to an illustrious predecessor and a personal quest for self-discovery. □

Josef Breitenbach
Spark of Life, New York 1946
Negative solarized silver print

Ruth Thorne-Thomsen
Dot Lady 1983
Manipulated Polaroid print

Herbert List
Untitled c. 1937
Gelatin silver print

Winifred Casson (laboratory work by Somerset Murray)
Untitled 1936
Gelatin silver print

Miro Svolík
My Wife c. 1985
Gelatin silver print

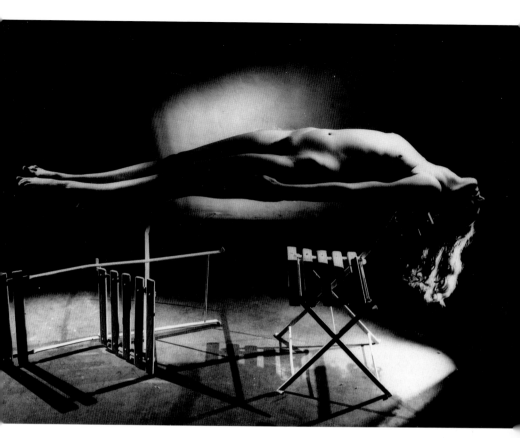

Lucien Lorelle
Catalepsie (Catalepsy) c. 1935-40
Gelatin silver print

Raoul Ubac
The Battle of Penthesileia c. 1930
Gelatin silver print

Hans Bellmer
La Poupée (*The Doll*) 1937
Hand-coloured silver print

David Salle
Untitled 1980-90
Gelatin silver print

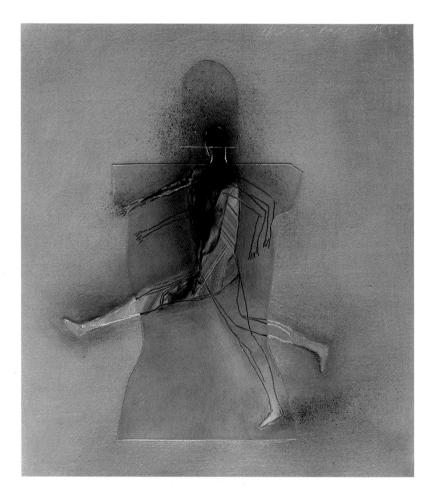

Holly Roberts
Man Running and Jumping 1991
Oil on silver print on canvas

Ron O'Donnell
Adam & Eve 1990
Construction/Cibachrome print

Kazimierz Podsadecki
Venus B 1933
Photomontage

Doug Prince
Anatomy Figure with Olive Tree 1993
Gelatin silver print

Vera Lehndorff + Holger Trülzsch
Oxydation from *Trans-figurations* 1986
Dye transfer

John Stezaker
Untitled 1990
Collage

Annette Messager
Mes Trophées (My Trophies) 1987
Acrylic, charcoal, pastel on black and white photographs

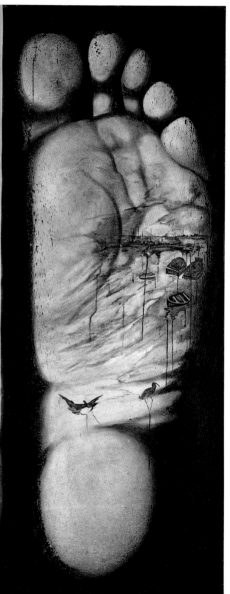

Jiři Stach
Remembering D.D. 1988
Colour transparency

Andre Racz
Newborn Bird #13 1943
Collage (halftone cutouts and ink)

Heinz Hajek-Halke
Double-exposure Nude and Street Scene c. 1927
Gelatin silver print

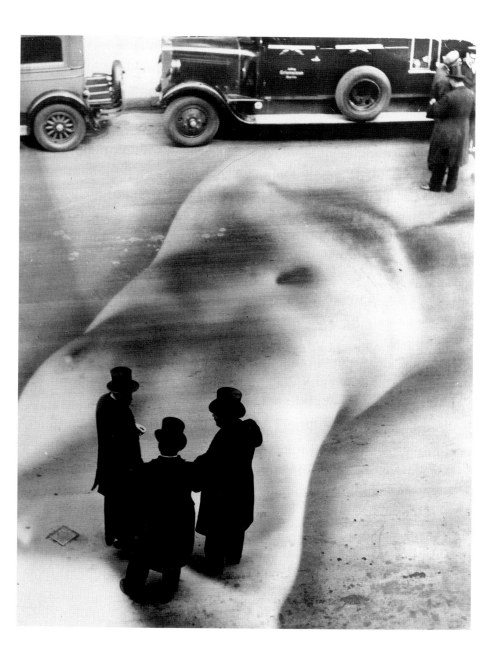

Gordon L. Bennett
Change in Time and Place 1988
Gelatin silver print and handcoloured postcard

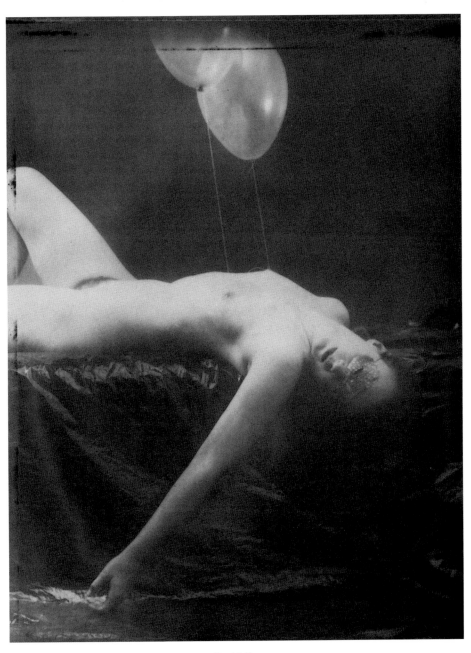

Pavel Baňka
Nude with Balloons 1985
Gelatin silver print

413

Karel Teige
Untitled 1941
Photocollage

Aleksander Krzywoblocki
Save Our Souls 1928
Collage

Joel-Peter Witkin
La Serpentine, Marseilles 1992
Gelatin silver print

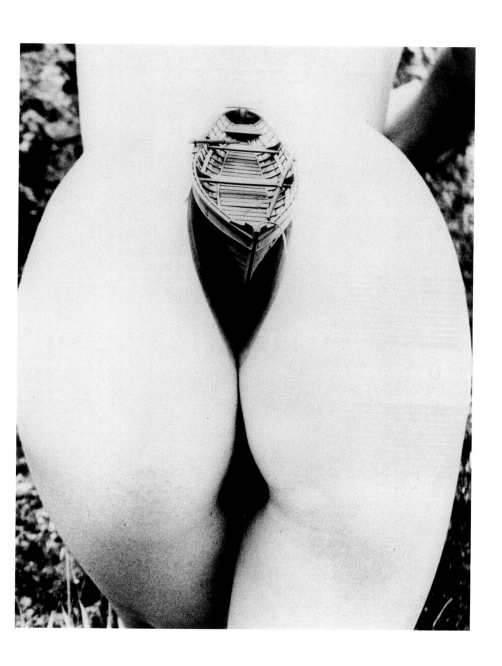

Minayoshi Takada
Untitled 1947-50
Toned gelatin silver print

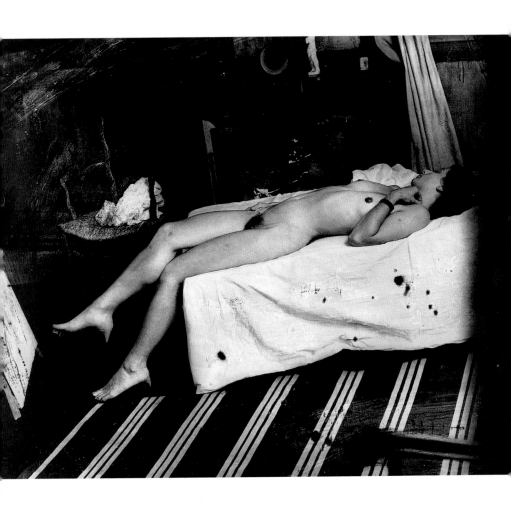

Joel-Peter Witkin
Nègre, Fetishist 1990
Gelatin silver print

(below)Rémy Fenzy
Untitled 1991
Selenium-toned gelatin silver print

(overleaf) Gary Schneider
Untitled handprint 1993
Toned gelatin silver print

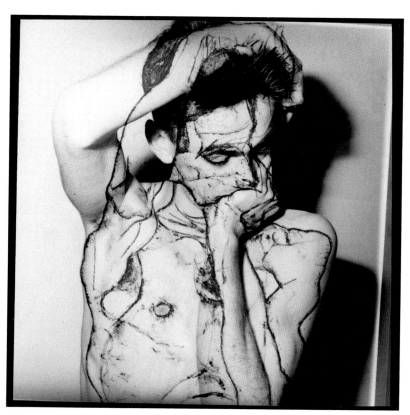

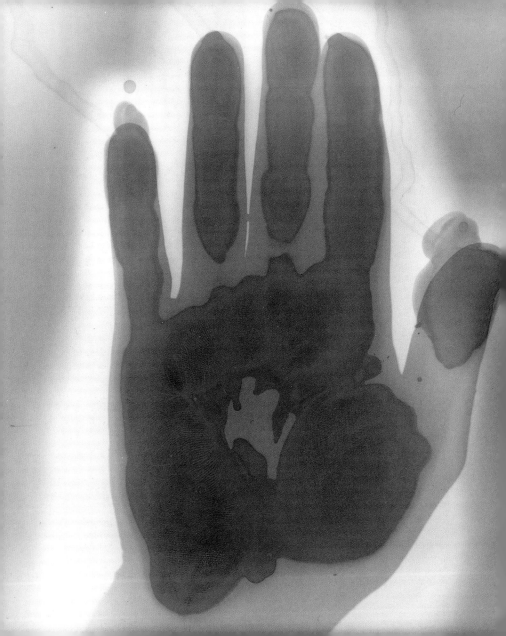

Notes

Abbreviation: *PN* = *Photographic News*

PREFACE: p. 9
1 Alice Jardine, 'Of Bodies and Technology', in Hal Foster, ed., *Discussions in Contemporary Culture*, Seattle, 1987, p. 157.

INTRODUCTION: p. 12
1 *PN*, 31 October 1879.
2 *PN*, 14 November 1879.
3 *PN*, 31 October 1879.
4 *Ibid.*
5 See C. Pinney, 'The Parallel Histories of Anthropology and Photography', in Elizabeth Andrews, ed., *Anthropology & Photography*, New Haven and London, 1992, pp. 80-81.
6 A report by the *Evening Standard* in 1865 described photography as 'the pioneer of all the physical sciences... Allied with chemistry and the microscope it seems destined to give us what we might almost style a new sense - a second sight.'
7 *PN*, 10 February 1888.
8 *Ibid.*
9 In Gail Buckland, *First Photographs*, New York, 1980, p. 163. Buckland cites persistent reports in the 1870s and 1880s claiming that a murder victim would have a portrait of the murderer and the scene of the crime etched as it were onto his or her retina. 'Negatives in the eye preserved by nature's camera', they were called by *PN* on 22 March 1889.
10 André Rouillé and Bernard Marbot, *Le Corps et son image*, Paris, 1986, pp. 73-75.
11 Anita Mozley, *Eadweard Muybridge: Muybridge's Complete Human and Animal Locomotion*, New York, Vol. I, 1979, p. xxxi.
12 François Dagognet, Etienne-Jules Marey, *A Passion for the Trace*, New York, 1992, p. 16.
13 *Ibid.*, p. 18.
14 *Ibid.*, p. 43.
15 *PN*, 3 June 1887.
16 *Rouillé* (note 10).
17 Mark Haworth-Booth, *The Golden Age of British Photography 1839-1900*, New York, 1984, p. 22.
18 For example, *Mes Modèles* (tri-monthly), A. Vignola, ed., Paris, 1906; *Le Nu ésthetique* (monthly), Emile Bayard, ed., Paris, 1902.
19 *PN*, 11 August 1865.
20 Jorge Lewinski, *The Naked and the Nude: A History of Nude Photography*, London, 1987, p. 59.
21 In Naomi Rosenblum, *A World History of Photography*, New York, 1984, p. 463.
22 The Remarque article appeared in *Sport im Bild* in 1928. Discussed by M. Ekstein in *The Rites of Spring*, Toronto, 1989, pp. 276-78.
23 'A Picture is Worth More than 1000 Words', *UHU* 3 (February 1926): 83.
24 Raoul Hausmann, 'La Composition dans la Photographie', in Roger Vulliez, ed., *Raoul Hausmann Photographies 1927-1957*, Paris, 1979, p. 7.
25 In Christopher Phillips, 'Resurrecting Vision: The New Photography in Europe between the Wars', in M. Hambourg and C. Phillips, *The New Vision: Photography between the World Wars*, New York, 1989, p. 77.
26 *Ibid.*, pp. 107-08.

FRAGMENTS: p. 32
1 Aaron Scharf, *Art and Photography*, London, 1974, p. 195.
2 Tracy Teslow, 'The Nineteenth Century: The Triumph of the Fragment', in *Caduceus* 8 (Autumn 1992): 47.
3 *Ibid.*
4 For a brief description of Sander's work in this area, see Maria Hambourg *et al.*, *The Waking Dream: Photography's First Century*, New York, 1993, p. 355.
5 In Jorge Molder, 'This is a History of a Body', in *John Coplans: A Self Portrait* (ex. cat.), Centro de Arte Moderna, Lisbon, 1992, p. 170.

FIGURES: p. 60
1 Stephen Kern, *Anatomy and Destiny: A Cultural History of the Human Body*, New York, 1974, p. 1.
2 *PN*, 26 November 1858.
3 A number of early daguerreotype nudes, both those intended as aids to artists and those expressly designed to titillate, are published in Stefan Richter, *The Art of the Daguerreotype*, London, 1989.
4 Aaron Scharf, *Art and Photography*, London, 1974, p. 119.
5 In Jorge Lewinski, *The Naked and the Nude: A History of Nude Photography*, London, 1987, p. 25.
6 *PN*, 9 January 1880.
7 The image may have been taken by the photographer and writer Charles Hose.
8 M. Macintyre and M. MacKenzie, 'Focal Length as an Analogue of Cultural Distance', in *Anthropology & Photography*, New Haven and London, 1992, pp. 162-63.
9 Sidney Allan, 'A Visit to Steichen's Studio', in Jonathan Green, *Camerawork: A Critical Anthology*, New York, 1973, pp. 28-32.
10 In W. Naef, *Edward Weston: The Home Spirit and Beyond*, The J. Paul Getty Museum, Malibu, California (ex. cat.), 1987, n.p.
11 Parks and Gregory were a husband and

wife team. See *Lewinski* (note 5), pp. 121-22.
12 In *Lewinski* (note 5), pp. 139-41.
13 Letter to the author, January 1993.
14 'I like the form of a cross, I like its proportions. I arrange things in a Catholic way,' quoted in David S. Rubin, *Cruciformed Images: Images of the Cross Since 1986* (ex. cat.), Cleveland Center for the Contemporary Arts, Cleveland, Ohio, 1991, p. 18.
15 Manuel Santos, 'Javier Vallhonrat: The Possessed Space', in *The Possessed Space*, Munich, 1992, p. 16.
16 Ingrid Sischy, *Lee Friedlander: Nudes*, London, 1991, n.p.

PROBES: p. 106
1 15 February 1866. And *PN* commented on 12 May 1875, 'Daily the microscopic journals bring us new discoveries.'
2 *PN*, 16 May 1879.
3 Maria Morris Hambourg *et al.*, *The Waking Dream: Photography's First Century*, New York, 1993, p. 275.
4 André Jammes, 'Duchenne de Boulogne, La Grimace Provoquée, et Nadar,' in *La Gazette des Beaux Arts 92* (December 1978). *PN* commented in July 1859 that his method resulted in a 'living anatomy'. Darwin was sufficiently intrigued by Duchenne's work (and the use of photography generally to freeze fleeting expressions) to make use of it to illustrate *The Expression of the Emotions in Man and Animals*, 1872. He also used O. G. Rejlander's photographs for the same purpose; such was the interest that they were 'copied into Continental Journals and scattered broadcast throughout the world' (*PN*, 2 May 1879).
5 André Jammes (note 4) has argued that Duchenne's work was 'contemporary with the argument as to whether beauty lies in immobility of the features or in a lively facial expression'.
6 *PN*, 5 November 1875.
7 This was the forerunner of the large photography departments in place in major hospitals today.
8 *PN*, 18 May 1888.
9 On 16 May 1879 *PN* reported an exhibition in Paris of 'a large number of photographs of the brain and skin in health and disease'. Generally nineteenth-century photographs have been ill-conserved, and poorly captioned and catalogued.
10 Even today there are areas in which drawing is preferred. See Simon Brown in *Professional Photographer*, Feb. 1993.
11 K. B. Roberts and J. D. W. Tomlinson, *The Fabric of the Body: European Traditions of*

Anatomical Illustration, Oxford, 1992, p. 612.
12 In discussion with the author.
13 Dr Lennart Nilssons' extraordinary achievement, reproduced in *LIFE* Magazine on 30 April 1965, 'The Drama of Life Before Birth', showed for the first time a living embryo inside the mother's womb. He used a specially built super-wide angle lens and a tiny flash-beam at the end of a surgical scope.
14 When G. N. Hounsfield invented computed tomography in 1972, for example, he had devised an innovative x-ray technology allowing for artifact-free images with a soft-tissue differentiation not previously possible with standard x-rays.
15 Magnetic resonance imaging, which creates its pictures by subjecting the body to a strong magnetic field, provides high-contrast images in any desired sectional orientation, and without the perils of ionizing radiation. Its strength is its capacity to show functioning systems, and soft tissue. It does not depict anatomy well.
16 Endoscopic imagery is still used for images of the living embryo within the womb because the genitals are too small to be viewed by ultrasound, x-ray or computer-aided visuals.
17 Roslyn Poignant, 'Surveying the Field of View: The Making of the RAI Photographic Collection,' in Elizabeth Edwards, ed., *Anthropology & Photography*, New Haven and London, 1992, p. 58.
18 *Ibid*, p. 55.
19 In Frank Spencer, 'Some Notes on the Attempt to Apply Photography to Anthropometry during the Second Half of the Nineteenth Century, in Edwards (note 17), pp. 99-100.
20 Donald Taylor, '"Very loveable human beings,": The Photography of Everard im Thurn', in Edwards (note 17), p. 189. Im Thurn's own more naturalistic photography showing people engaged in their daily pursuits would point the way for the more humane cultural relativism of the twentieth century.
21 2 August 1885.
22 *PN*, 9 March 1889.

FLESH: p. 138
1 Paul Valéry, *L'Idée Fixe, ou deux hommes à la mer*, Paris 1933.
2 In Arno Rafael Minkkinen, ed., *Elegant Intimacy*, Retretti Art Centre, Finland, 1993, p. 28.

PROWESS: p. 166
1 In Alisdair Foster, *Behold the Man: The Male Nude in Photography* (ex. cat.), Stills Gallery, Edinburgh, 1988, p. 11.

2 The photographs resulted from an informal impromptu session conducted one afternoon at Graham's mother's house in California.
3 William A. Ewing, *Breaking Bounds: The Dance Photography of Lois Greenfield*, London, 1992, pp. 99-117.
4 *Ibid.*, p.14.

EROS: p. 206
1 *PN*, 11 August 1865.
2 *PN*, 26 November 1858.
3 Erwin Blumenfeld, *My Hundred Best Photos*, New York, 1979, p. 25.
4 I am indebted to Vince Aletti of New York for guidance in this area as well as for access to his collection.

ESTRANGEMENT: p. 238
1 Paul Virilio, *War and Cinema: The Logistics of Perception*, London, 1989.
2 *PN*, 6 August 1880.
3 *Ibid.*
4 *The Philadelphia Reporter*, January 1872.
5 Letter to the author, October 1993.
6 In Sarah Graham-Brown, *Images of Women: The Portrayal of Women in Photography of the Middle East 1860-1950*, London, 1988, p. 135.

IDOLS: p. 272
1 Naomi Wolf, *The Beauty Myth*, London, 1990, p. 10.
2 *The Philadelphia Reporter*, January 1872.
3 *PN*, 29 August 1879.
4 For a discussion of the work of Desbonnet, see *Accord à corps: Edmond Desbonnet et la culture physique de la collection Desbonnet*, Paris, 1993.

MIRROR: p. 294
1 Rejlander's reticence to expose himself, in both the literal and figurative senses, unwittingly reflects his attitudes to photography itself, which he believed achieved its potential only when 'clothed' in the high-minded idealism of both morality and art.
2 In 1990 Brunenberg produced a booklet on the series *Immagini Scoperte*. Introduction by W. K. Coumans. Weert, Holland.
3 In Adam Weinberg, ed. *Vanishing Presence* (ex. cat.), Walker Art Center, Minneapolis/ Rizzoli, New York, 1989, p. 123.
4 Max Kozloff, 'The Etherealized Figure and the Dream of Wisdom,' in Adam Weinberg (note 3), p. 38.
5 For an early synopsis of key body artists, see *Bodyworks* (ex. cat.), Museum of Contemporary Art, Chicago, March 8–April 27, 1975 (introductory essay by Ira Licht). See

also Willoughby Sharp, 'Body: A Pre-Critical Non-Definitive - the Human Body or Parts' in *Avalanche* (Fall 1970): 14-17.
6 Letter to the author, November 1993.
7 Johannes Birringer, 'Imprints and Re-Visions: Carolee Schneemann's Visual Archeology', in *Performing Arts Journal 15* (May 1993): 31-46.

POLITIC: p. 324
1 Marina Warner, *Monuments and Maidens: The Allegory of the Female Form*, London, 1985, p. 295.
2 See Mike Mandel, *Making Good Time: Scientific Management, the Gilbreths, Photography and Motion, Futurism*, Mike Mandel, Santa Cruz, California, 1989.
3 Letter to the author, October 1993.
4 *De Light: Helen Chadwick* (ex. cat.), Institute of Contemporary Art, University of Pennsylvania, Philadelphia, Pa., 1991, n.p.

METAMORPHOSIS: p. 354
1 Anne Wilkes Tucker, *Unknown Territory: Photographs by Ray K. Metzker*, New York, 1984, p. 15.
2 Letter to the author, September 1993.
3 Jean-Paul Sartre, *Nausea* (trans. from French), London, 1965, p. 143-44.
4 Derek Bennett, 'Ernestine Ruben: A Vocabulary of the Senses,' in *Ernestine Ruben: Photographs*, Zurich/Frankfurt/Düsseldorf, 1989, p. 12.

MIND: p. 386
1 Quoted in Peter Webb, *The Erotic Arts*, London, 1975, p. 369.
2 Vera Lehndorff and Holger Trülzsch, '*Veruschka' Transfigurations*, London, 1986, p. 146.
3 *Ibid.*
4 *Annette Messager, comédie tragédie 1971-1989* (ex. cat.), Musée de Grenoble, 1989-90, p. 144.
5 *Ibid.*
6 Letter to the author, January 1994, citing the photographer's thoughts and those of Régis Durand.
7 Aragon also wrote 'Today the crowds are returning to art through the photographs – with the excited gestures of children at play...' in M. Hambourg and C. Phillips, *The New Vision: Photography between the World Wars*, New York, 1989, p. 144.
8 William A. Rossi, *The Sex Life of the Foot and Shoe*, Belmont, Calif., 1989. Cited in conversation with the author.
9 In conversation with the author, February 1993.

Sources of Illustrations

Preliminary pages Dr David Phillips: A single spermatozoon fertilizing a human egg, 1992; Courtesy: Dr David Phillips/Science Photo Library, London. Anonymous: Endoscopic image of the hand of a human foetus *in vivo* after 3 months, 1985; Courtesy: Petit Format/ Nestle/Science Photo Library, London. Alexander Tsiaras: Endoscopic image of the foot of a human foetus *in vivo* after 11 weeks; Courtesy: Science Photo Library, London.
8 © 1971 Arnulf Rainer; Courtesy: Galerie Ulysses, Vienna **11** © 1992 Andres Serrano; Courtesy: Paula Cooper Gallery, New York **13** Courtesy: The Wellcome Institute Library, London **17** Courtesy: Noel Chanan and June Stanier, London **19** Courtesy: The Wellcome Institute Library, London **24** Courtesy: Royal Photographic Society, Bath, England **29** © Estate of George Platt Lynes, New York; Courtesy: Estate of George Platt Lynes **30** Courtesy: Science Photo Library, London **33** Courtesy: Bibliothèque Nationale, Paris **35** Courtesy: Mitchell Kennerly Papers, Rare Book and Manuscript Division, New York Public Library **36** Courtesy: Bibliothèque Nationale, Paris **37** International Museum of Photography at George Eastman House, Rochester, New York **38** © 1981 Estate of Robert Mapplethorpe; Courtesy: Estate of Robert Mapplethorpe **39** © 1981 Arizona Board of Regents, Center for Creative Photography, Tucson, Arizona; Courtesy: The J. Paul Getty Museum, Malibu, California **40** Courtesy: Houk Friedman Gallery, New York **41** © 1987 Ernestine Ruben; Courtesy: The artist, New York **42** Courtesy: Musée National d'Art Moderne, Centre Georges Pompidou, Paris **43** © ICT, Berkeley, California; Courtesy: The Imogen Cunningham Trust, Berkeley, California **44** © 1987 Pierre Radisic; Courtesy: The artist, Brussels **45** © 1987 Ernestine Ruben; Courtesy: The artist, New York **46** © 1978 Lynn Davis; Courtesy: The artist, New York **47** © 1983 Pierre Radisic; Courtesy: The artist, Brussels **48, 49** © 1992 Robert Davies; Courtesy: The artist, London **50** © 1979 David Buckland; Courtesy: The artist, London **51** © 1984 John Coplans; Courtesy: The artist, New York **52** © 1991 Tono Stano; Courtesy: The artist, Prague **53** Copyright © J-P Kernot; Courtesy: Sotheby's, London **54** © 1978 Lynn Davis; Courtesy: The artist, New York **55** © 1981 Arizona Board of Regents, Center for Creative Photography, Tucson, Arizona; Courtesy: Sotheby's, London **56** © 1986 Pierre Radisic; Courtesy: The artist, Brussels **57** © 1985 John Coplans; Courtesy: The artist, New York **58** © 1991 Tono Stano; Courtesy: The artist, Prague **59** © 1984 John Coplans; Courtesy: The artist, New York **61** Courtesy: The J. Paul Getty Museum, Malibu, California **65** © Stefan Richter/All Rights Reserved; Courtesy: Stefan Richter, Reutlingen, Germany **66** Courtesy: Bibliothèque Nationale, Paris **67** Courtesy: Private Collection, London **68** Courtesy: The Board of Trustees of the Victoria & Albert Museum, London **69, 70, 71** Courtesy: Bibliothèque Nationale, Paris **72** Courtesy: Collection Gérard Lévy, Paris **73** Courtesy: The Board of Trustees of the Victoria & Albert Museum, London **74** Courtesy: Bibliothèque Nationale, Paris **75** Courtesy: National Portrait Gallery, London **76** Courtesy: Royal Anthropological Institute, London **77** Courtesy: Private Collection, London **78** Courtesy: Houk Friedman Gallery, New York **79** Courtesy: The J. Paul Getty Museum, Malibu, California **80** © 1993 Michel Frizot; Courtesy: Michel Frizot, Paris **81** Courtesy: Sotheby's, London **82** © Stefan Richter/All Rights Reserved; Courtesy: Stefan Richter, Reutlingen, Germany **83** Courtesy: Vince Aletti, New York **84** Courtesy: The J. Paul Getty Museum, Malibu, California **85** © 1952 Horst P. Horst; Courtesy: The artist, New York **86, 87** Courtesy: Sotheby's, London **88** Courtesy: Marina Schinz, New York **89** Courtesy: International Museum of Photography at George Eastman House, Rochester, New York **90** Courtesy: Private Collection, London **91** © 1994 Artists Rights Society (ARS), New York/V.G. Bild-Kunst, Bonn; Courtesy: Musée National d'Art Moderne, Centre Georges Pompidou, Paris **92** © ICT, Berkeley, California; Courtesy: Imogen Cunningham Trust, Berkeley, California **93** © 1981 Arizona Board of Regents, Center for Creative Photography, Tucson, Arizona; Courtesy: The J. Paul Getty Museum, California **94** © 1983 Estate of Robert Mapplethorpe; Courtesy: Estate of Robert Mapplethorpe, New York **95** Courtesy: Private Collection, London **96** © 1994 Artists Rights Society (ARS), New York/ADAGP/Man Ray Trust, Paris; Courtesy: Houk Friedman Gallery, New York **97** © 1978 Lee Friedlander; Courtesy: Fraenkel Gallery, San Francisco **98** © 1963 Ruth Bernhard; Courtesy: Sotheby's, London **99** © 1984 Estate of Robert Mapplethorpe; Courtesy: Estate of Robert Mapplethorpe **100** © 1950 Horst P. Horst; Courtesy: The artist, New York **101** © 1975 Dianora

Niccolini; Courtesy: The artist, New York
102 © 1992 Philip Trager; Courtesy: The
artist, Fairfield, Connecticut 103 © 1991
Sally Mann; Courtesy: The artist and Houk
Friedman Gallery, New York 104 © 1990
Humberto Rivas; Courtesy: The artist,
Barcelona 105 © 1987 Javier Vallhonrat;
Courtesy: The artist, Madrid 107 Courtesy:
Musée Beaune, Beaune, France
111 Courtesy: Sotheby's, London
114 Courtesy: The Wellcome Institute
Library, London 115 Courtesy: The Board of
Trustees of the Victoria & Albert Museum,
London 116 Courtesy: Noel Chanan and
June Stanier, London 117 Courtesy: Private
Collection, London 118 Courtesy: Musée
Beaune, Beaune, France 119 Courtesy:
Private Collection, London 120 Courtesy:
Siemens, Erlangen, Germany 121 © 1977
Ralph Hutchings; Courtesy: The artist,
London 122 Courtesy: The Wellcome
Institute Library, London 123 Courtesy:
Ecole nationale supérieure des beaux arts,
Paris 124, 125 © 1985 Ralph Hutchings;
Courtesy: The artist, London
126, 127 Courtesy: The Royal
Anthropological Institute, London
128 Courtesy: Petit Format/Nestle/Science
Photo Library, London 129 Courtesy:
Genesis Films/Science Photo Library, London
130 Courtesy: CNRI/Science Photo Library,
London 131-133 Department of Anatomy,
University 'La Sapienza', Rome/Science Photo
Library, London 134-136 Courtesy: Science
Photo Library, London 137 © Harold
Edgerton; Courtesy: Houk Friedman Gallery,
New York 139 © 1984 John Coplans;
Courtesy: The artist, New York
140, 141 © 1992 Robert Davies; Courtesy:
The artist, London 144, 145 © 1994 Artists
Rights Society (ARS), New York/ADAGP,
Paris; Courtesy: Musée National d'Art
Moderne, Centre Georges Pompidou, Paris
146, 147 Courtesy: Houk Friedman Gallery,
New York 148 © 1994 Harry Callahan;
Courtesy: Pace/MacGill Gallery, New York
149 © ICT, Berkeley, California; Courtesy:
Imogen Cunningham Trust, Berkeley,
California 150 © 1991 Regina DeLuise;
Courtesy: Bonni Benrubi Gallery, New York
151 © 1984 Chuck Close; Courtesy: Pace/
MacGill Gallery, New York 152 © 1981
Regina DeLuise; Courtesy: Bonni Benrubi
Gallery, New York 153 © 1980 Jed Devine;
Courtesy: Bonni Benrubi Gallery, New York
154 © 1992 Sally Mann; Courtesy: The artist
and Houk Friedman Gallery, New York
155 © 1990 Sally Mann; Courtesy: The artist
and Houk Friedman Gallery, New York

156 © 1984 John Coplans; Courtesy: The
artist, New York 157 © 1973 Emmet Gowin;
Courtesy: Pace/MacGill Gallery, New York
158 © 1992 Jock Sturges; Courtesy: The
artist, San Francisco, California 159 © 1987
Jock Sturges; Courtesy: The artist, San
Francisco, California 160 © 1989 Jock
Sturges; Courtesy: The artist, San Francisco,
California 161 © 1981 Richard Sadler;
Courtesy: The artist, Coventry, England
162 © 1984 Pierre Radisic; Courtesy: The
artist, Brussels 163 © 1984 Ernestine Ruben;
Courtesy: The artist, Princeton, New Jersey
164, 165 © 1985 Yves Trémorin; Courtesy:
The artist, Saint-Malo, France 167 Courtesy:
Private Collection, London 171 © Prof. E.
Desbonnet; Courtesy: Amicale E. Desbonnet,
Sèvres, France 172 Courtesy: Private
Collection, London 173 © ICT, Berkeley,
California; Courtesy: Imogen Cunningham
Trust, Berkeley, California 174 Courtesy:
Royal Photographic Society, Bath
175 Courtesy: Private Collection, London
176 Courtesy: The Wellcome Institute
Library, London 177, 178 Courtesy: Michel
Frizot, Paris 179 Courtesy: The Library of
Congress, Washington, D.C. 180 Courtesy:
Vince Aletti, New York 181 © 1989 Mary
Ellen Mark; Courtesy: The artist, New York
182 Courtesy: Michel Frizot, Paris
183 Courtesy: George Rodger, Kent, England
184 Courtesy: Private Collection, London
185 © Association des Amis de J. H.
Lartigue; Courtesy: La Mission du Patrimoine
Photographique, Paris 186 © Ministère de la
Culture, France; Courtesy: La Mission du
Patrimoine Photographique, Paris
187 © 1972 Ken Heyman; Courtesy: The
artist, New York 188 Courtesy: Michel
Frizot, Paris 189, 190 Courtesy: The Library
of Congress, Washington, D.C.
191 Courtesy: Houk Friedman Gallery, New
York 192 © Estate of Herbert List,
Hamburg; Courtesy: Private Collection,
London 193 Courtesy: Peter Webb, London
194 © 1990 Danielle Weil; Courtesy:
The artist, New York 195 Courtesy: *Harpers
& Queen* Magazine, London
196, 197 Courtesy: The Library of Congress,
Washington, D.C. 198 © 1965 Leon
Levinstein; Courtesy: Howard Greenberg
Gallery, New York 199 © 1982 Helen Levitt;
Courtesy: Laurence Miller Gallery, New York
200 © 1982 Estate of Robert Mapplethorpe;
Courtesy: Estate of Robert Mapplethorpe
201 Courtesy: Vince Aletti, New York
202 © Estate of Aaron Siskind, New York;
Courtesy: Vince Aletti, New York
203 © 1992 Philip Trager; Courtesy: The

425

artist, Fairfield, Connecticut 204 Courtesy: Private Collection, London 205 © 1992 Lois Greenfield; Courtesy: The artist, New York 207 Courtesy: Marina Schinz, New York 211 Courtesy: The J. Paul Getty Museum, Malibu, California 212 Courtesy: Bibliothèque Nationale, Paris 213 Courtesy: Sotheby's, London 214 Courtesy: International Musuem of Photography at George Eastman House, Rochester, New York 215 Courtesy: Bibliothèque Nationale, Paris 216, 217 Courtesy: Howard Greenberg Gallery, London 218 Courtesy: Collection Gérard Lévy & François Lepage, Paris 219 © 1993 Monas Hierogliphica, Milan; Courtesy: Monas Hierogliphica, Milan 220, 221 Courtesy: Private Collection, London 222 Courtesy: Collection François Lepage, Paris 223 Courtesy: Vince Aletti, New York 224 Courtesy: Collection Gérard Lévy & François Lepage, Paris 225 © 1993 Monas Hierogliphica, Milan; Courtesy: Monas Hierogliphica, Milan 226, 227 © Estate of James Abbe, New York; Courtesy: Washburn Gallery, New York 228, 229 © 1993 Monas Hierogliphica, Milan; Courtesy: Monas Hierogliphica, Milan 230 © 1955 George S. Zimbel; Courtesy: The artist, Montreal, Quebec 231 Courtesy: Musée National d'Art Moderne, Centre Georges Pompidou, Paris 232 © 1994 Artists Rights Society (ARS), New York/SPADEM, Paris; Courtesy: Musée National d'Art Moderne, Centre Georges Pompidou, Paris 233-235 Courtesy: Vince Aletti, New York 236 © 1986 Ralph Gibson; Courtesy: The artist, New York 237 © 1993 Lucien Clergue; Courtesy: The artist, Arles, France 241 Courtesy: Royal Anthropological Institute, London 242 Courtesy: Sotheby's, London 243 Courtesy: Bibliothèque Nationale, Paris 244, 245 left and right Courtesy: The Wellcome Institute Library, London 246, 247 Courtesy: The Library of Congress, Washington, D.C. 248 © 1993 Monas Hierogliphica, Milan; Courtesy: Monas Hierogliphica, Milan 249 Courtesy: Roger Viollet, Paris 250 Courtesy: Collection Gérard Lévy, Paris 251 Courtesy: Collection Gérard Lévy & François Lepage, Paris 252 Courtesy: Private Collection, London 253 Courtesy: Collection Gérard Lévy & François Lepage, Paris 254 Courtesy: Stanley B. Burns, MD & The Burns Archive, New York 255, 256 Courtesy: The Wellcome Institute Library, London 257 Courtesy: Stanley B. Burns, MD & The Burns Archive, New York 258, 259 Courtesy: The Wellcome Institute Library, London 260 Courtesy:

Collection Gérard Lévy, Paris 261 Courtesy: Collection Gérard Lévy & François Lepage, Paris 262-263 Courtesy: The Wellcome Institute Library, London 264 Courtesy: Collection Gérard Lévy & François Lepage, Paris 265 © 1989 Stefan Richter/All Rights Reserved; Courtesy: Stefan Richter, Reutlingen, Germany 266 Courtesy: Musée National d'Art Moderne, Centre Georges Pompidou, Paris 267 © 1993 Lee Miller Archives; Courtesy: Lee Miller Archives, Sussex, England 268 © 1972 Jeffrey Silverthorne; Courtesy: The artist, South Bend, Indiana 269 © 1975 Antonin Kratochvil; Courtesy: The artist, New York 270, 271 © 1987 Diane Michener; Courtesy: Pace/MacGill Gallery, New York 273 Courtesy: Library of Congress, Washington, D.C. 275, 276 Courtesy: Private Collection, London 277-279 © Prof. E. Desbonnet; Courtesy: Amicale E. Desbonnet, Sèvres, Paris 280, 281 Courtesy: Gordon L. Bennett, Kentfield, California 284-285 Courtesy: Private Collection, London 286 © 1985 The Estate of Robert Mapplethorpe; Courtesy: The Estate of Robert Mapplethorpe 287, 288 Courtesy: Private Collection, London 289 © 1979 Burt Glinn; Courtesy: Magnum, New York 290 © Lynne Cohen; Courtesy: PPOW Gallery, New York 291 Courtesy: Horst P. Horst 292 © 1984 Max Yavno; Courtesy: The G. Ray Hawkins Gallery, Los Angeles 293 © 1990 Herb Ritts; Courtesy: Fahey Klein Gallery, Los Angeles 295 Courtesy: The Royal Photographic Society, London 297 Courtesy: Private Collection, London 298 © 1978 Lucas Samaras; Courtesy: Pace/MacGill Gallery, New York 299 © 1990 Lucas Samaras; Courtesy: Pace/MacGill Gallery, New York 301 © 1994 Robert Morris/Artists Rights Society (ARS), New York; Courtesy: Leo Castelli Gallery, New York 302, 303 © 1963-91 Carolee Schneemann; Courtesy: The artist, New York 304 © 1994 Bruce Nauman/ Artists Rights Society (ARS), New York; Courtesy: Leo Castelli Gallery, New York 305 above © 1984 Henry Lewis; Courtesy: Baudoin Lebon, Paris 305 below © 1980 Henry Lewis; Courtesy: Baudoin Lebon, Paris 306 © 1974 Andrzej Rozycki; Courtesy: The artist, Warsaw 307 © Suzy Lake; Courtesy: The artist, Toronto 308, 309 above © 1984 Michel Szulc-Krzyzanowski; Courtesy: The artist, Amsterdam 308, 309 below © 1980 Michel Szulc-Krzyzanowski; Courtesy: The artist, Amsterdam 310 © 1992 Arno Rafael Minkkinen; Courtesy: The artist, Andover,

Massachusetts 311 © 1973 Arno Rafael Minkkinen; Courtesy: The artist, Andover, Massachusetts 312, 313 © 1985 Alain Fleischer; Courtesy: Musée National d'Art Moderne, Centre Georges Pompidou, Paris 314 © 1977 Dieter Appelt; Courtesy: Kicken/Pauseback Gallery, Cologne 315 © 1979 Dieter Appelt; Courtesy: Kicken/Pauseback Gallery, Cologne 316 © 1977 Dieter Appelt; Courtesy: Kicken/Pauseback Gallery, Cologne 317 © 1978 Dieter Appelt; Courtesy: Kicken/Pauseback Gallery, Cologne 318, 319 Courtesy: Musée National d'Art Moderne, Centre Georges Pompidou, Paris 320, 321 © 1989 Jo Brunenberg; Courtesy: The artist, Weert, Holland 322 © 1977 The Estate of Francesca Woodman; Courtesy: George and Betty Woodman, New York 323 © 1980 The Estate of Francesca Woodman; Courtesy: George and Betty Woodman, New York 325 © 1987 Jana Sterbak; Courtesy: René Blouin Gallery, Montreal 326 Courtesy: Private Collection, London 327 © 1993 Monas Hierogliphica, Milan; Courtesy: Monas Hierogliphica, Milan 328, 329 Courtesy: The Library of Congress, Washington, D.C. 330 Courtesy: Adam J. Boxer, New York 331 © 1990 Kathy Grove; Courtesy: The artist and Pace/MacGill Gallery, New York 332 © 1982 Nancy Burson; Courtesy: Jayne H. Baum Gallery, New York 333 *left* © 1983-84 Nancy Burson; Courtesy: Jayne H. Baum Gallery, New York 333 *right* © 1984 Nancy Burson; Courtesy: Jayne H. Baum Gallery, New York 336 © 1991 Annie Sprinkle; Courtesy: The Torch Gallery, Amsterdam 337 © 1989 Barbara Kruger Collection: Edye/Eli Broad, Los Angeles, California; Courtesy: Mary Boone Gallery, New York 338 © 1994 Richard Hamilton/Artists Rights Society (ARS), New York; Courtesy: The artist, Oxford, England 339 © 1976 Robert Walker; Courtesy: The artist, Montreal, Quebec 340 © 1974 Robert Heinecken; Courtesy: Pace/MacGill Gallery, New York 341 © 1993 Michelle Bradford; Courtesy: The artist, Surrey, England 342 © 1989 Helen Chadwick; Courtesy: The artist, London 343 © 1990 Helen Chadwick; Courtesy: The artist, London 344 © 1990 Cindy Sherman; Courtesy: The artist and Metro Pictures, New York 345 © 1979 Carolee Schneemann; Courtesy: The artist, New York 346 © 1986 Lorna Simpson Collection: Suzanne and Howard Feldman; Courtesy: Josh Baer Gallery, New York 347 © 1991 Lorna Simpson Collection: J. B. Speed Art Museum, Louisville, Kentucky;

Courtesy: Josh Baer Gallery, New York 348 © 1990 Laurie Simmons; Courtesy: The artist and Metro Pictures, New York 349 © 1977 Cindy Sherman; Courtesy: The artist and Metro Pictures, New York 350 © 1993 Matuschka; Courtesy: The artist, New York 351 From copy transparency 352 © 1984 Mike Mandel; Courtesy: The artist, Santa Cruz, California 353 © 1990 Lynne Cohen; Courtesy: PPOW Gallery, New York 355 Copyright © J-P Kernot; Courtesy: Houk Friedman Gallery, New York 359 © 1988 Ralph Gibson; Courtesy: The artist, New York 360 Courtesy: Marina Schinz, New York 361 André Kertész © Ministère de la Culture, France; Courtesy: Houk Friedman Gallery, New York 362 André Kertész © Ministère de la Culture, France; Courtesy: Sotheby's, London 363 © 1986 Florence Chevallier; Courtesy: The artist, Saint-Saëns, France 364 © 1985 Florence Chevallier; Courtesy: The artist, Saint-Saëns, France 365 © 1993 Wilhelm Helg; Courtesy: The artist, Geneva, France 366 © 1987 Pierre Radisic; Courtesy: The artist, Brussels 367 © 1990 Ray K. Metzker; Courtesy: The artist and Laurence Miller Gallery, New York 368, 369 © 1988 Holly Wright; Courtesy: The artist, Charlottesville, Virginia 370, 371 © 1993 Doug Prince; Courtesy: The artist, Portsmouth, New Hampshire 372 © 1986 Emmet Gowin; Courtesy: The artist and Pace/MacGill Gallery, New York 373 © 1958 Harry Callahan; Courtesy: The artist and Pace/MacGill Gallery, New York 374 © 1986 Jacqueline Feldine; Courtesy: The artist, Ville d'Avray, France 375 © 1988 Jacqueline Feldine; Courtesy: The artist, Ville d'Avray, France 376, 377 © 1988 Holly Wright; Courtesy: The artist, Charlottesville, Virginia 378 © 1981 Ernestine Ruben; Courtesy: The artist, New York 379 Courtesy: Marina Schinz, New York 380, 381 © 1965 Barbara Crane; Courtesy: The artist, Chicago 382 Courtesy: Houk Friedman Gallery, New York 383 © 1994 Artists Rights Society (ARS), New York/ADAGP/ Man Ray Trust, Paris; Courtesy: Houk Friedman Gallery, New York 384 © 1992 George Woodman; Courtesy: The artist, New York 385 © 1992 Tono Stano; Courtesy: The artist, Prague 387 Courtesy: Gordon L. Bennett, Kentfield, California 388, 389 Courtesy: Library of Congress, Washington, D.C. 393 Courtesy: Houk Friedman Gallery, London 394 © 1983 Ruth Thorne-Thomsen; Courtesy: The artist and Laurence Miller Gallery, New York 395 © Estate of Herbert

427

List, Hamburg; Courtesy: Private Collection, London 396 Courtesy: Private Collection, London 397 © 1985 Miro Svolík; Courtesy: The artist, Prague 398 © 1994 Artists Rights Society (ARS), New York/ADAGP, Paris; Courtesy: Musée National d'Art Moderne, Centre Georges Pompidou, Paris 399 Courtesy: Musée National d'Art Moderne, Centre Georges Pompidou, Paris 400 © 1994 Artists Rights Society (ARS), New York/ ADAGP, Paris; Courtesy: Houk Friedman Gallery, New York 401 © 1990 David Salle; Courtesy: Robert Miller Gallery, New York 402 © 1991 Holly Roberts; Courtesy: The artist, Charlottesville, Virginia 403 © 1990 Ron O'Donnell; Courtesy: The artist, Edinburgh 404 Courtesy: Private collection, London 405 © 1993 Doug Prince; Courtesy: The artist, Portsmouth, New Hampshire 406 © 1986 Vera Lehndorff and Holger Trülzsch; Courtesy: The artists, Paris 407 © 1990 John Stezaker; Courtesy: The artist, London 408 © 1987 Annette Messager; Courtesy: Galerie Crousel-Robelin Bama, Paris 409 © 1980 Jiři Stach; Courtesy: The artist, Prague 410 Courtesy: Adam J. Boxer, Brooklyn, New York 411 Courtesy: Sotheby's, London 412 © 1988 Gordon L. Bennett; Courtesy: The artist, Kentfield, California 413 © 1985 Pavel Baňka; Courtesy: The artist, Prague 414 Courtesy: The Czech Museum of Literature, Prague 415 Private collection, London 416 © 1992 Joel-Peter Witkin; Courtesy: Pace/MacGill Gallery, New York 417 Courtesy: Houk Friedman Gallery, New York 418 © 1990 Joel-Peter Witkin; Courtesy: Pace/MacGill Gallery, New York 419 © 1991 Rémy Fenzy; Courtesy: The artist, Solre-le-château, France 420 © 1993 Gary Schneider; Courtesy: PPOW Gallery, New York

Acknowledgments

First of all I wish to thank the following photographers and artists who have generously contributed their work to this book: Dieter Appelt, Pavel Baňka, Gordon L. Bennett, Ruth Bernhard, Michelle Bradford, Jo Brunenberg, David Buckland, Nancy Burson, Harry Callahan, Helen Chadwick, Florence Chevallier, Lucien Clergue, Chuck Close, Lynne Cohen, John Coplans, Barbara Crane, Robert Davies, Lynn Davis, Regina DeLuise, Jed Devine, Jacqueline Feldine, Rémy Fenzy, Alain Fleischer, Lee Friedlander, Ralph Gibson, Burt Glinn, Emmet Gowin, Lois Greenfield, Kathy Grove, Richard Hamilton, Robert Heinecken, Wilhelm Helg, Ken Heyman, Horst P. Horst, Ralph Hutchings, Antonin Kratochvil, Barbara Kruger, Suzy Lake, Vera Lehndorff, Helen Levitt, Henry Lewis, Sally Mann, Mary Ellen Mark, Matuschka, Annette Messager, Ray K. Metzker, Diane Michener, Arno Rafael Minkkinen, Robert Morris, Bruce Nauman, Dianora Niccolini, Ron O'Donnell, Doug Prince, Pierre Radisic, Arnulf Rainer, Stefan Richter, Herb Ritts, Humberto Rivas, Holly Roberts, Andrzej Rozycki, Ernestine Ruben, Richard Sadler, David Salle, Lucas Samaras, Carolee Schneemann, Gary Schneider, Cindy Sherman, Jeffrey Silverthorne, Laurie Simmons, Lorna Simpson, Annie Sprinkle, Jiři Stach, Tono Stano, Jana Sterbak, John Stezaker, Jock Sturges, Miro Svolík, Michel Szulc-Krzyzanowski, Ruth Thorne-Thomsen, Philip Trager, Yves Trémorin, Holger Trülzsch, Javier Vallhonrat, Robert Walker, Danielle Weil, Joel-Peter Witkin, George Woodman, Holly Wright, Max Yavno, George Zimbel.

I am deeply grateful for the assistance and support I have received from my professional acquaintances in galleries, museums, libraries and the like. Without their knowledge, generosity and enthusiasm the project would never have been possible: Kathryn Abbe, Paris; Vince Aletti, New York; Ken Arnold, London; Regula Arreger, New York; Susan Arthur, New York; Josh Baer, New York; Gordon Baldin, Los Angeles; Jayne H. Baum, New York; Jonathan Benthall, London; Vladimir Birgus, Prague; Kathleen and Henry Blumenfeld, Paris; Pierre Bonhomme, Paris; David Brady, London; Susan Brundage, New York; Dr Stanley B. Burns; Carole Callow, Sussex; Andy Clarke, London; Bernard Cormerais, Sèvres, France; Chantal Crousel, Paris; Urszula Czartoryska, Lodz, Poland; Julie Dinsdale, London; Amanda L. Doenitz, San Francisco;

Catherine Draycott, London; Gary Evans, London; David Fahey, Los Angeles; Alisdair Foster, Edinburgh; Barry Friedman, New York; Michel Frizot, Paris; Philippe Garner, Sotheby's, London; Dr W. Gedroyc, London; Howard Greenberg, New York; Ina Gutmann, Vienna; Vicki Harris, New York; Mark Haworth-Booth, London; Paul Heyer, Vancouver; Edwynn Houk, New York; Margaret Kelly, New York; Rudi Kicken, Cologne; Kathy Lando, New York; Jasmine Landry, Montreal; Jean-Claude Lemagny, Paris; François Lepage, Paris; Marian Leuba, Beaune, France; Gérard Lévy, Paris; Thomas Lyons, New York; Peter MacGill, New York; Frances Mclaughlin-Gill, Nicolas Monti, Milan; Bernard Marbot, Paris; C. Mathon, Paris; Weston Naef, Los Angeles; Wendy Olsoff, New York; Ron and Elizabeth Partridge, Berkeley, California; Priska Pasquer, Cologne; Terence Pepper, London; Frederick Petzel, New York; Penny Pilkington, New York; Marc Pitre, Montreal; Amy Poll, New York; Howard Read, New York; Alain Sayag, Paris; Max Scheler, Hamburg; William Schupbach, London; David Spear, New York; Ethaline Staley, New York; Will Stapp, Rochester, New York; Richard Tardiff, New York; Leslie Tonkonow, New York; Dr Richard Underwood; Julie van Haaften, New York; Ron Warren, New York; Peter Webb, London; Sophie Webel, Paris; Gabrielle Wimmer, Vienna; Anna Winand, New York; Taki Wise, New York; David Wooters, New York; Chris Wright, New York.

I wish to thank the following museums, libraries, galleries and collectors for their generous help in locating imagery and arranging permissions for reproduction: The Estate of James Abbe, New York; Vince Aletti, New York; Jayne H. Baum Gallery, New York; Gordon L. Bennett Collection, Kentfield, California; Bonni Benrubi Gallery, New York; Bibliothèque Nationale, Paris; René Blouin Gallery, Montreal; Mary Boone Gallery, New York; Adam J. Boxer, New York; Bill Brandt Estate, London; Stanley B. Burns, MD & The Burns Archive, New York; Leo Castelli Gallery, New York; Noel Chanan and June Stanier, London; Imogen Cunningham Trust, Berkeley, California; The Czech Museum of Literature, Prague; Edmond Desbonnet Collection, Sèvres, France; Anthony d'Offay Gallery, London; Ecole nationale supérieure des beaux arts, Paris; Fahey Klein Gallery, Los Angeles; Fraenkel Gallery, San Francisco; Houk Friedman Gallery, New York; Michel Frizot Collection, Paris; Galerie Baudoin-Lebon, Paris; Galerie Crousel-Robelin Bama, Paris; Galerie Ulysses, Vienna; International Museum of Photography at George Eastman House, Rochester, New York; The J. Paul Getty Museum, Malibu, California; Howard Greenberg Gallery, New York; G. Ray Hawkins Gallery, Los Angeles; Estate of André Kertész, New York; Kicken/Pauseback Gallery, Cologne; François Lepage Collection, Paris; Gérard Lévy Collection, Paris; Library of Congress, Washington, D.C.; Magnum, New York; Estate of Man Ray, Paris; Estate of Robert Mapplethorpe, New York; Metro Pictures, New York; Lee Miller Archives, London; Laurence Miller Gallery, New York; Mission du Patrimoine Photographique, Paris; Monas Hierogliphica, Milan; Musée Beaune, Beaune, France; Musée National d'Art Moderne, Centre Georges Pompidou, Paris; The National Portrait Gallery, London; New York Public Library; Pace/MacGill Gallery, New York; PPOW Gallery, New York; Stefan Richter Collection, Reutlingen, Germany; The Royal Anthropological Institute, London; Marina Schinz Collection, New York; Science Photo Library, London; Siemens Corporation, Erlangen, Germany; Sotheby's, London; The Victoria & Albert Museum, London; Roger Viollet, Paris; Peter Webb Collection, Paris; Wellcome Institute for the History of Medicine, London; Estate of Francesca Woodman, New York.

Finally, I wish to thank my wife, Clare. Her comments on the text and image selection were always to the point and her support and encouragement never wavered.

Index